Parables from (a not quite) Paradise, NV 89154

v.2 The History News Network Essays

"World Peace Could Be at Hand—If Only We Could Be more like the Sloth."

By

William N. Thompson

Preface by Richard Shenkman

1st Books Library
Bloomington, IN

This book is a work of non-fiction. Names and places have been changed to protect the privacy of all individuals. The events and situations are true.

© 2003 by William N. Thompson. All rights reserved.

No part of this book may be reproduced, stored in a retrieval system, or transmitted by any means, electronic, mechanical, photocopying, recording, or otherwise, without written permission from the author.

ISBN: 1-4107-9190-4 (e-book)
ISBN: 1-4107-9189-0 (Paperback)

Library of Congress Control Number: 2003096599

This book is printed on acid-free paper.

Printed in the United States of America
Bloomington, IN

1stBooks – rev. 11/19/03

Preface

Bill Thompson is a rara avis among political scientists. He knows how to tell a story. My favorite is the one he told a few years ago about a fellow he ran into in Britain. They fell into a conversation about Margaret Thatcher and Ronald Reagan, the British fellow insisting that Thatcher was a far better leader than Reagan. The implication of course was that this reflected well on Britain. Thompson's droll response? Reagan proves that in America we don't need leaders.

I hope I have the story right in all its details but probably don't. As the social scientists have demonstrated in numerous studies, every time we tell a story we reinvent it, shaping the narrative to incorporate information we have acquired in the interim. But I am confident I have got the main theme correct and that is what is important.

Which brings me back to Bill Thompson. Like a novelist or a good historian he has the ability to tell a story which one wants to remember. How many political scientists can match him? Not many, I'm afraid. Most of the erudite papers political scientists write are forgotten almost immediately, even when they shouldn't be. I often wonder if the authors are writing for their readers or simply for themselves. It would seem that it is for themselves and if that's the case, fine. Writing is one of the best ways to educate oneself, forcing the brain to grapple with the lumps in one's thinking, smoothing them out the way one would a bed sheet.

But when I read Bill Thompson, I am always conscious that he is conscious of his reader. He writes for the benefit of the reader. As a devoted reader of his work—for years I have had the pleasure of publishing his essays, first on TomPaine.com and then on HistoryNewsNetwork.org—I am grateful to him. He is always easy to read.

This takes talent. It also takes hard work. It's hard to write an essay which is fresh and interesting. Try it. You'll see. At Harvard Daniel Aaron would tell graduate students that easy writing makes hard reading. I always think of Aaron's comment when reading Bill's essays. You just know he worked hard on those essays.

As his editor for many years I was always a little shocked at how quickly he could turn out an essay. But the essays were always based on hard work. Unlike many writers, he'd done his hard thinking before he sat down to write.

Of course, you cannot write an essay unless you have something to say. And that brings me to another of Bill's strengths. He has something worthwhile to say about a great number of topics. His range is astonishing. While his scholarly work has to do with the gambling industry—that's the gambling industry, not the gaming industry as he points out in one piece—he can ably address politics and history too.

Dan Aaron had another aphorism. He said that we remember what is important. Thompson writes in a way that makes the reader remember. As I sat down to write this preface I realized that I could easily recall points Bill had made in essay after essay, as if I had just read them the other day rather than years before. I particularly was taken with his defense of Warren Harding. Harding always ranks among the bottom of presidents and with good reason. But Bill managed to make a case for him.

But enough of what I gleaned from Bill. Turn the page. As they say in the old Victorian novels, Dear Reader, it's time for you to find out.

Richard Shenkman
Seattle
June 2003

Contents

Preface iii

Introduction and Acknowledgements vii

1. World Peace Could Be At Hand—If We Could Only Be More Like the Sloth.. 1
2. What About "W" and that Pretzel, Anyway... 7
3. Three Heart Beats Away: "They" Nearly Made James Eastland President of the United States of America.. 11
4. I got My Job through Affirmative Action--And I was a Forty Year Old White Male 22
5. The Biggest Affirmative Action Program of All..................................... 27
6. 9-11 Not Victims –towers.. 31
7. The Worst Day in American History... 35
7a. John Beatty: "And Now For the Rest of the Story"--Maybe 39
8. St. Clair, Little Turtle, Little Crow, Little Six and Retribution 43
9. The Olympics Circles in Jerusalem 48
10. Olympics Carter Olympics Beijing 53
11. A Conservative Supports Reparations 57
12. Fugimori--Another Type of Reparations 64
13. Hiroshima Reflections 71
14. Being Number One Means Never Having to Say You're Sorry: a Panama Picture 78
15. Warren G. Harding--It Time for a Eulogy.. 82
16. Rating Presidential Greatness--Ratings Bunk 88
17. On Tricks and Stones and Nixon's Foul Mouth 90
18. Insinuations of Bigotry--Continuing 96
19. There's a Reason We Blow Up History in Las Vegas........................... 100
20. Like the District of Columbia Needs A(nother) Casino 105
21. The Government Can't Fill the Potholes, But it Can Give Us Powerball? Dah! 108
22. If Gambling Entrepreneurs took their Product to the F.D.A. 113
23. A Childhood Thought of a Lucky Las Vegas Resident........................ 118
24. Abolish the Office of Attorney General 120
25. The Ironies of a Nuclear state.. 126
26. The Concept of Nullification: The Latest Round 133
27. Two Things Nevada Can Be Proud of: Put Them on the Coin 139
28. Moralistic Politics Die in California... 143
29. Jeffords Bad, Jeffords Good: A Partisan Republican View................. 149
30. Pork Barrel Comes to White Pine County 153
31. Red, White, and Blue...Long May It Wave 157
32. God's Grace, Your Goodness.. 161

Introduction

In 1999 Richard Shenkman wrote to me and asked me to express my views on a few topics for a new e-journal he had created. He called it TomPaine.com(mon sense). He seemed to like my commentary, so he asked me to continue writing. I continued to write for him after he started a new venture called The History News Network. Similarly, almost like "out of the blue" Florence Rogers, the Program Manager, of KNPR Public Radio in Las Vegas asked me to make a commentary on some aspect of Nevada politics. I obliged, and again, I was asked to make more commentaries. In some cases I abstracted my radio commentaries from longer pieces I wrote for the History News Network. I set forth my radio commentaries in Volume One of <u>Parables from Paradise</u>. In this second volume I offer many of the essays I have written for the History News Network. There are others as well. All of them can also be accessed in their original form through the archives of the network at www.historynewsnetwork.org. However, I have kept the editing of the originals to a minimum for this volume. In a few cases (e.g., "The Sloth" "Three Heart Beats Away," "Long May it Wave, and "The Ironies of a Nuclear State") I am including here longer (HNN) versions of essays that also appeared as commentaries and are included in Volume One. The source date of each essay is recorded at its conclusion. (HNN means HistoryNews Network—HNN.com, while TP means TomPaine.com[mon sense]).

One of my essays ("The Worst Day in American History") prompted a very interesting response from Dr. Bill Luken, and with his permission I am including it after the essay. I am also including an essay ("Abolish the Office of Attorney General") I wrote for the <u>Kalamazoo Gazette</u> during the midst of the Watergate crisis. It conveys notions I gained from several years of research on the office of attorney general, the topic of my doctoral dissertation. I have also put in a previously unpublished piece ("Pork Barrel Comes to White Pine County") I wrote in 1984 after I accompanied a United States senator on a tour of small Nevada towns. He came bearing gifts from Washington, but was blessed with a reception totally unexpected.

Additionally I include a "Childhood Thought" about gambling—a thought that still haunts me (sometimes). The book ends with a poem of grace that appears in my book (co-author Anthony J. Juliano), <u>Heart Lines and Lyrics from Billy Gamble</u> (1st Books, 2003).

My thanks extend outward in many directions. First to those who inspired many of these essays simply by requesting that they be written—Richard Shenkman and Flo Rogers. Second to others that inspired efforts to dig for information that might generate ideas and expressions. University and research colleagues of many years and overseas hosts during many travels are numerous and collectively acknowledged, as they know whatever good comes in my words, I could not have done it by myself. Friends and special friends I call family especially Kay, Laura, Tim, Carmenza, Steve and Siqin continue always to be motivators and ones who inspire.

Thanks also are given to the staff of 1st Books Library, especially Lori Watterson and Vid Beldavs, for their diligent work in preparing the manuscript.

Parables from (a not quite) Paradise, NV 89154

1. World Peace Could Be At Hand—If We Could Only Be More Like the Sloth

In July 2002, I made a seventeen day tour of Peru. I ventured to ancient Cuzco and the exotic Inca fortress at Machu Picchu. I spent several days on the Amazon visiting Indian villages and hiking through the "selva." My final days were in the capital of Lima. It is always refreshing to escape the day to day life of the United States with its almost claustrophobic feelings brought about by the media's incessant accounts of turmoil and strife. Actually, for almost three weeks I heard nothing of skirmishes in Afghanistan, homicidal Palestinian bombers in Israel, Israeli tanks in Palestine, impending war in Iraq, lingering strife in Northern Ireland. No messages of conflict between congressional Democrats and a Republican president reached my ears.

Was I in Nirvana? In Machu Picchu and in the jungle, or as it is called locally, the "selva," I began to feel that perhaps I was, but then I did come back to reality in Lima. The city was engulfed in protests and strikes. The traffic was brutal. A stop sign or red light only meant that one would yield to bigger cars or trucks. A go sign or green light meant precisely the same thing. Pollution was horrific. Black soot flowed from each vehicle (actually newer cars spewed forth white smoke, perhaps in hopes of the election of a new pope). Horns blasted forth every conceivable kind of loud sound. At every corner, beggars approached car windows, as did persons selling everything from national flags and household cleaners, to candy and chewing gum. Squeegee blades were on stopped windows almost immediately. The beach suburb of Miraflores looked almost like a southern European resort, but the thought of the temporary shacks astride the surrounding mountains, made any feel of luxury or comfort rather uncomfortable. Each city, town, and suburb also found traffic flowing toward a central plaza—The Plaza de Armes—which celebrated Peru's role in the wars of the 1870s with neighbors

Ecuador, Chile, and Bolivia. A heavenly Nirvana it was not. But then, just maybe a heavenly Nirvana was near at hand.

Human society, and especially Western society, embraces an ethic of progress. The ethic is reflected in the biblical admonition that mankind should go forth and subdue the land for its own enrichment. Christian and Muslim principles (indeed misinterpreted but certainly acted upon) alike suggest that the faithful should go and convert the heathen, and trample them (even to death) if they resist the "true word." Western individualism is often a playing out of a win-lose game of social Darwinism. Militarism is a natural concomitant of human group value structures. Yet most faiths also envision a quite different Nirvana, an almost non-materialistic "pot of gold," at the end of the rainbow we call life. In contrast with the images of CNN and the street scenes of Lima, the heaven we seem to wish to seek is one of satisfaction, relaxation, non-competition, non-acquisition but still self sufficiency, self pleasures of perhaps undefined natures (but then of very well defined nature for suicide bombers, ala 70 virgins at one's feet), and above all, most of all, always always PEACE. That ultimate desire of Peace is also the central virtue espoused in diplomatic circles and in foreign policy statements of all nations. That ultimate desire of Peace is the rationale for international conferences, and it is the rationale for the creation of bi-lateral and multi-lateral alliances, and of course, for the creation of the United Nations.

In the selva I sensed that this Nirvana was alive and well on our own earth. The naturalist guide for our Amazon boat tours, urged us to be quiet, but to get our cameras out. He was sure he had spotted among the leaves of a Kapok tree, a three-toed sloth. Indeed he had, and we sat in stunned silence as he directed our eyes to the upper branches to what appeared to be a lump on the truck of the tree. After we took our pictures and moved onward in our journey, the guide told us about this most heavenly of all God's creatures.

As the story unfolded, I indeed was convinced that the key to our human survival, the key to peace on earth could be displayed in the lifestyle of this much maligned creature.

The sloth is not a taker. The mammal, which typically grows to be about 8 pounds and as much as two feet in body length, does not engage in any win-lose or parasitic games. As the sloth survives, it harms no other living creature. He eats only the leaves of very specific trees, deriving both nutritional substance and its water needs from the foliage. Yet the sloth gives back to the trees and to other creatures as well. He exists in a symbiotic and synergistic relationship with all others in the environment of the few trees that he occupies.

The sloth has a hairy body, and the hair becomes a breeding ground for the algae of the region. The algae in turn give the body of the sloth a greenish coloring pattern that affords him a camouflaged hiding from predators. While the sloth spends most of its time hanging in sleep in mid level branches of its trees, it does seek energy from the sun by rising to higher limbs. The sunshine, in turn, gives valuable heat to the algae as well, helping sustain their growth.

The long stringing hair of the sloth is also the residential home of a special sloth moth. With its limited dietary needs (the sloth craves only what it needs, unlike human beings, not what it wants), the sloth needs to engage in the animal process of discarding wastes only once a week. In the process of doing so, he descends the tree, very slowly, digs a hole, deposits the waste and in an environmentally correct nice manner covers up the hole when he is done. However as the waste is being deposited, the sloth moth also deposits eggs in the fecal material. The burial of the waste then protects the eggs. As the eggs are now nurtured to produce a new generation of moths, the soils about the waste have been enriched by it, and so are able to better feed the tree that gives the sloth its home and its very limited food supply.

The sloth is very vulnerable to the animals which prey upon it, notable the harpy eagle and the jaguar. The sloth has sharp claws which can be used in defense. They are never used as offensive weapons. The animals greatest protection comes from its ability to hide. It seeks middle level branches which are out of reach of the jaguar and also below a range of convenience for flight by the harpy eagle. The acts of stealth are aided by the camouflage coloring and also by the sloth's ability to remain still for hours and hours at a time. The animal sleeps in an upside down position hanging from limbs of the tree for as many as 20 hours every day.

The sloth is in its most dangerous position when it descends the tree to do its weekly duty. The sloth does not have a muscular capacity to make any kind of escape when it is on the ground. It is the slowest of all mammals. Its legs cannot move it, instead it pulls itself along the ground at a rate of a few feet per hour. On the other hand, the long arms of the sloth enable the animal to swim with great ability, especially with a speed that can take the sloth away from pursuing jaguars. Naturally in its jungle environment it gravitates to trees that are near watered areas.

The natural strengths (rather the lack thereof—it has the least muscle mass of any mammal) of the sloth incline it toward an complete aversion to any conflict within its own population. It has very few and very simple needs and no wants. The sloth will inhabit only a few trees during its lifetime. It will bond with these trees and mark them with its individual smells. The others of the species will respect its trees, and in turn it is not at all motivated to seek out trees belonging to others of its kind. There are reports that during mating "season" (a stretch of the word), two male two toed sloths may fight for a female's affection, however, the three toed variety are rarely so inclined. The sloths are solitary creatures that spend almost their entire lifetimes alone in the midst of their individual trees. The concept of group based battles is totally out of the realm of contemplation for these animals.

Males and females of other species (ergo, homo sapiens) do have their episodes of group battles, but again this cannot be the case with the sloths. With this species, male female relationships have advanced to an extremely wonderful level not found with other animals (hopefully this is not just a chauvinistic male perspective). Male and female sloths meet for only three days a year. It takes the animals three days to engage in the mating act. (From a female perspective the idea of three days of pre-activity should seem to be rather advanced behavior from males). After the three days the male retreats to his tree, dreaming about the moment during his long episodes of sleep. Well, of course, the female is left with a burden, but it is not overwhelming. A period of gestation lasts six months, and most of this time the female is sleeping and just hanging around her tree. After birth, the young sloth clings to the mother for about two months, observing the slow cycle of activity. It is then taken to a tree of its own and released. The female then, like the male, can enjoy four to five months of solitude.

In two Indian villages of the Amazon, our tour group observed that young native girls had pet sloths. The animals clung around their waists, much as babies were tied in cloth around the waists of the older women. The pets were exceedingly loving, and craved to be held. Members of our group took turns holding the sloths, always being careful to avoid contact with the claws. The notion struck this observer that perhaps the sloth could be brought into the culture of Lima and also the United States. The animal could be offered as a surrogate child for young teenagers that otherwise might be having real babies. Perhaps, the teenage girls could carry sloths until they reached an appropriate age when they could give more adequate care to real babies. As the sloths may live to be as old as thirty years, they could be passed on from one girl to another in new rites of passage. Not only could we learn from the sloth, but this giving animal could make great contributions to our society in direct ways as well.

In the lexicon of man, the sloth has been much abused. Religions that seek peace have overlooked this species almost unique contribution. Instead, the sloth has been set forth as a model for one of the seven deadly sins—laziness. This is unkind, and unjustified. When we go to sleep we pray for peace. We envision a heaven that is much like the peaceful world of the sloth. Lazy? What do we think of all day—ways to take advantage of others and then ways to avoid conflict with others. The sloth probably dreams our dreams as well, wakes up, looks around, and sees that indeed, the dreamed-of Nirvana is at hand. So it goes back to sleep. Why not?

The central prophet and creative spirit of the most prominent religion of the western world offered the words that should elevate the sloth to a position if not of worship itself, at least of emulation, "It is more blessed to give…." World peace could be at hand. If only mankind could be more like the sloth.

    HNN, July 29, 2002

2. What About "W" and that Pretzel, Anyway

There is a frivolous side of presidential history as the eight year reign of Bill Clinton may attest. Even in times of war, a light moment may be savored. Perhaps there is comic relief (let's hope so given the satisfactory outcome) in the headlines regarding George W's episode of choking on a bow tie (or was it butterfly) shaped pretzel while watching the football playoffs in the White House. Bush had the sense not to be entertaining himself alone as he was accompanied by his vigilant and trustful family dog. He chewed but he did not swallow. It is a relief that we can dispel rumors that he may have started drinking again. (Rumors I have heard from at least five credible Democrat sources). If he would have exercised good judgement he certainly would have had a beer or two to make the pretzels go down his esophagus smoothly.

The recent near tragedy in the White House brings to my mind other recent episodes of presidential dangers that arose from unusual situations or places. Leaving out Bill Clinton (our memories are too fresh regarding his episodes), I would like to reflect on a few of these.

Jerry Ford was the only president who had a genuine career as an outstanding athlete. He was an All-Big Ten lineman with the University of Michigan football team in the mid-1930s. To win honors as the most valuable player on his team, he certainly had to be physically coordinated. Yet on June 1, 1975, he slipped an fell down the stairs as he was deplaning Air Force One. Then later that year on Christmas Day he fell and nearly hit a tree while skiing at Vail, Colorado. He was an accomplished skier—most of the time.

Former President Lyndon Johnson liked to suggest that Ford's rather slow and thoughtful demeanor in Question and Answer situations indicated he was dimwitted ("He played football too often without a helmet." "He couldn't count to eleven without…."). Yet it wasn't always his physical stumbles that got him into danger. There was that remark in his debate with Jimmy Carter about how (in 1976)

Poland was "free." That might have been the difference in the election campaign.

But then there was Jimmy Carter. Carter was a physical fitness advocate and the first of several presidents who enjoyed competitive jogging. On September 15, 1979, he was competing in a 10,000 meter road race in the Maryland mountains near Camp David. While it was a normal activity for a 55 year old man, it had dire consequences on that hot day. The President collapsed in a faint.

Ah! But when Carter really needed his physical prowess, he was up to the task, and we as a nation can give thanks for that. It was probably the highlight of his entire term. On April 20, 1979, President Carter choose to go fishing on a pond near his home in Plains, Georgia. He wanted to relax, "lay back," wiggle the worm on the hook, and just enjoy the silent afternoon—by himself. He overruled secret service objections and rowed the boat onto the pond all by himself. They could only watch in horror from the banks as the historical events unfolded. Carter was just relaxing and sensing the pleasures of the springtime breeze, when suddenly, out of nowhere appeared a killer rabbit. The rabbit swam toward the president's boat, its teeth snarling and a menacing look in its eyes. The rabbit attacked the boat, but quickly with artistic athletic acumen, our president grabbed an oar and lifted it high before striking it down on the vicious intruder. He beat the rabbit back, without tipping the boat over, and the rabbit retreated, as the secret service stood helplessly with guns drawn and binoculars in hand.

To most keen observers of the presidential scene these would appear to be but isolated events never to be mentioned again outside of a parlor game of trivia. However, a pattern of explanation is available to explain why each such event occurred. The pattern may also be utilized by President Bush and his successors if they wish to avoid reoccurrences. The explanation is offered with the proverbial "grain of salt," and with a reminder that Johnny Carson always started his "Ripley Believe it or Not," segments with—the admonition that Ripley did say "or NOT."

Parables from (a not quite) Paradise, NV 89154

My discovery of the truth behind the events began when I saw a biorhythm calculator on sale for $14.95 at Radio Shack. I made the purchase and read up on the science of biorhythms. At birth we release the beginnings of three waves or rhythms. A physical rhythm lasts 23 days, an intellectual rhythm 28 days, and an intellectual rhythm lasts 33 days. For the first part of the wave we are "high" on the factor, then we experience a dangerous or "critical" cross over day, and we are then low for the second part of the wave. Ergo, we are physically high for 11 days, have a critical cross over day, we are low for eleven days, cross-over day, then high again, ad infinitum for a lifetime.

Explanations for the presidential crises we have witnessed: On June 1, 1975, Ford was high emotionally, but he was low intellectually, and this is the main one—he was low physically. On December 25, 1975, he was also low physically and emotionally, but he was high intellectually. So what did the All-Big Ten footballer do on his physically high days—he engages in presidential debates and says stupid things. Of course, during his debate with Carter on October 6, 1976, he was intellectually low.

Carter was at the physical bottom of his rhythms when he collapsed jogging. When he decided to go fishing alone against the wishes of the secret service he was intellectually low, and his emotionally low rhythms certainly impeded his gaining sense of possible danger in the pond. But, alas, at the critical moment when he successfully fought off the attacking rabbit he enjoyed an extra degree of strength from the fact that he was physically high on his biorhythm charts.

So what about George W? On January 13, 2002 he was 20280 days old. He had experienced 614 intellectual wave cycles, but he was in the 18th day of his current cycle. He was intellectually low, having been just one day removed from his intellectually critical day. Someone else should have chosen his diet for him on that day. The choice of pretzels without beer (or even diet cola) was a very bad decision. He had experienced 724 emotional cycles, and he was on the eighth day of a new cycle. Emotionally he was high, and it is good he was, as he choose to have his trusting dogs nearby for the impending emergency. But the important explaining rhythm was the physical one. He had had 881 cycles over his fifty-five plus years, and he was on the 17th day of his latest cycle. He was low physically. His esophagus was not in top condition to handle the pretzel, especially a pretzel without a beer.

So can biorhythms be used for serious historical analysis? Why not?

On July 16, 1973 Alexander Butterfield told Sam Ervin's Watergate Committee that President Richard Nixon had installed voice recording machines in the Oval Office. Nixon was intellectually low that day. He did nothing. For one week he did nothing. Then on July 23, Special Prosecutor Archibald Cox subpoenaed the tape recordings. At that moment Nixon was on an intellectually critical day. His last chance to destroy the tapes without committing a criminal offense passed him by as he could not make an office saving decision. Historians have sought to find the date that Nixon installed the tape recording devices. Until this moment they have not found the precise time. Butterfield suggested that the recorders were installed in the Spring of 1971. He was close. They were installed on March 18, 1971. On that day, Richard Milhouse Nixon was 58 years and 68 days old. All of his rhythms were aligned, all three were at their most critical cross over day. It is quite possible that Nixon not only decided to install the taping devices that day, but he probably had a "good feeling" about it, and I suspect he probably climbed the ladder himself to put the machinery into the ceiling boards. As Johnny Carson said, you can "Believe it" or "NOT."

HNN, January 22, 2002

Parables from (a not quite) Paradise, NV 89154

3. Three Heart Beats Away: "They"Almost Made James Eastland the President of the United States of America

A Presidential Election

'Tis the season for reflection (not again, ugh). Some wish to turn the clock back to 1980, others to the 1948 election, or to 1947. I'd like to start this historical journey in 1972, July 28th to be precise. 10 a.m. By that time in American history, our nation had well learned that segregation was wrong, yet we also knew that some of our political leaders were not yet repentant regarding their past (and contemporary) wrongs. Martin Luther King had been dead for over four years, but George Wallace was still in the midst of a quest to win influence in national politics, an influence decidedly adverse to the cause of civil rights.

So at the appointed hour, an election is to take place. An election for president. Let's see, there are two candidates. Republican Senator Hugh Scott of Pennsylvania has put forth to name of Senator George Aiken for president. Aiken is a Vietnam war skeptic ("We should declare victory and leave"), and a liberal as far as Republicans go. He has consistently supported the cause of civil rights. (www.uvn.edu/~dceweb/aiken).

The senate majority leader, Democrat Mike Mansfield puts forth his party's candidate for president. His candidate is James Eastland, a senator from Mississippi. Eastland is a patriot (in terms of the Vietnam conflict), a conservative, and an outspoken (and unrepentant) champion of racial segregation in America.

Eastland had addressed a rally of the White Citizens Council in 1956 saying, "When in the course of human events it becomes necessary to abolish the Negro race, proper methods should be used. Among these are guns, bows and arrows, slingshots and knives…"(Quoted by historian Robert Caro, www.wikipedia.org/wiki/James_Eastland).

And the winner is....With the votes of senators with names such as McGovern, Kennedy (Teddy), Mansfield, Muskie, Fulbright, Jackson, Humphrey, Hart (Phil), Ervin and the rest of the Democratic senate (majority) contingent it is clear cut: Senator James Eastland is elected President.

Hypothetical, a fantasy. Absolutely not. Check out page 25905 of the Congressional Record, July 28, 1972. The office was not the President of the United States (the office sought by Strom Thurmond in 1948), but rather the President Pro Tempore of the United States Senate. But then, that office was not too far removed from the White House—it was just three heart beats away.

The liberal Democrat establishment actually choose to place James Eastland in a position to be the President of the United States, if there but was an accident or disaster. Just think, perhaps the vice presidency could have been vacated by a scandal, then James Eastland would only be two heart beats away from the presidency as a result of the votes of the Democrat liberal establishment. Perhaps, the president himself could have been engrossed in a scandal that could have led to a resignation, or maybe the president could have had a serious health crisis—maybe a phlebitis attack causing his total disability or death. Then the Democrat liberal establishment would have put James Eastland but a single heartbeat away from being president. The one heart beat could have been that of a Speaker of the House who had had a major heart attack, say, maybe six years before. How close was James Eastland to becoming our President? Do the names Agnew, Nixon, and Albert have any meaning? Close! (Albert, 1990. Little Giant. Univ. Oklahoma Press, p. 372)

On the other hand, there could be an assassination or a terrorist attack. These things can happen, you know. Tragically, after September 11, we know very well that these kinds of things DO happen. If they had happened thirty years ago, the Democrat liberal establishment of the United States Senate would have caused James Eastland to be the President of the United States of America.

Parables from (a not quite) Paradise, NV 89154

Senator James Eastland served as the President Pro Tempore of the United States Senate, three heart beats from the presidency of the United States for six years—until he left the Senate in 1979.

This is not to place blame on Democrats alone (although they love to do the reverse). In 1981, January 5, 10 a.m. to be precise, there was another election. Republican Senators did elect Strom Thurmond President Pro Tempore of the United States Senate. Their new majority gave them him the victory over the candidate of the Democratic establishment. Minority leader Robert Byrd of West Virginia had nominated another senator on behalf of his liberal colleagues. A good solid representative of the civil rights movement? A Kennedy, a Levin, a Bayh, a Proxmire, a Biden? No the Democrat candidate was Senator John Stennis, another segregationist from Mississippi.

Thurmond served as president pro tempore from 1981 through 1987, when the Democrat majority did elect Stennis.

Stennis served for two years until he left the senate. A member of the house of representatives named Trent Lott took the Stennis seat in the senate, but being in the minority party, he did not become president pro tempore. Indeed, we should recognize that Mr. Lott's arrival in the senate resulted in the position of president pro tempore being taken away from his segregationist state. The new president pro tempore in 1987 was Byrd, a former member of the Ku Klux Klan, who still used the "N" word in public. Byrd and Thurmond traded the office back and forth until the end of 2002, each taking their turns at being but "three heartbeats away" from actually holding the presidency of the United States of America. Their place was given to each by the acquiescence of the senators from their parties—liberals, moderates, and conservatives.

A Paradox

I find it totally incredulous that a senator has been driven out of a leadership position because he suggested that someone the ilks of a Thurmond, and Eastland, or a Stennis or Byrd might have made a good president, when the full membership of the Senate had actually voted to make these individuals given a tragic accident, attack, or illnesses (or scandal) the president of the United States of America. Yet I have never heard one word of condemnation of a Kennedy or a Kerry or a Levin for what had to be totally stupid votes to elevate abject segregationists to positions so near to the epicenter of power in the United States.

Yet my Democrat friends—who had told me they wished Trent Lott to remain majority leader because it would help them in the 2004 election—told me also that the position of president pro tempore is really just a figure head, honorary position given to the oldest senator of the majority party, that the office means nothing. WRONG! The office is "three heart beats away."

Beginnings of the Position—The Early Phase—Duties

The position of president pro tempore is established in the United States Constitution. The words "pro tempore," simply mean "for the time being." Article I, Section 5 proclaims that the senate shall chose "a president pro tempore, in the absence of the vice president, or when he (the vice president) shall exercise the office of president of the United States."

The constitution also gave congress the power to determine who should hold the powers of the presidency if that office and the office of vice president are both vacant. In 1792—congress determined that the president pro tempore would be the person that would exercise the powers of the presidency in such a situation. In turn, if the president pro tempore was not available, the powers would pass to the speaker of the house of representatives. In early years the president pro tempore was given extra powers regarding committee appointments, but soon these powers were removed so that the position was simply one with presiding functions—and of course a position in the line of succession.

Until 1890, the position was filled only when the senate was in session, as this was the only time it would be necessary for a senator to preside over the body. An extreme danger lurked in the land as a result. When congress was adjourned during several presidencies, the country was without an heir apparent should something have happen to the president: during the presidencies of James Madison (whose vice president, Eldbrige Gerry had died in 1814), Andrew Jackson (because of the resignation of John Calhoun as vice president), John Tyler (who was a vice president who succeeded to the presidency on the death of William Henry Harrison), Millard Fillmore (who ascended to the presidency on death of Zachary Taylor), Franklin Pierce (whose vice president William King died shortly after inauguration), Andrew Johnson (who succeeded Abraham Lincoln), Grant (whose vice president, Henry Wilson, died in his second term), Arthur (who ascended to the presidency after the assassination of James Garfield), Grover Cleveland (whose vice president Thomas Hendricks died in the first year of his first term). The unspeakable almost did happen. John Tyler was aboard a yacht that experienced an explosion. He survived but two cabinet members were killed—we did come that close to having the crisis of a vacancy with no designated successor.

The realization that there was no legally designated person to take over the presidency during part of Cleveland's term led the next Congress to change the order of succession. In 1886 congress reviewed succession and took the president pro tempore and speaker of the house off the list.

In the 94 years when the president pro tempore was but two heart beats away (and in the cases indicated above when there was no vice president, but one heart beat away), 55 senators occupied the post. One served before 1792. The first president pro tempore of the senate was Senator John Langdon of New Hampshire. During the second congress when the 1792 succession act was passed the post was held by Langdon and Richard Henry Lee of Virginia. The 53 other names on the list are for the most part not distinguishable to casual observers of American history—names like Jacob Reed of South Carolina, John Laurence of New York, Abraham Baldwin of

Georgia, Jesse Franklin of North Carolina, and Andrew Gregg of Pennsylvania.

But some interesting names also appear. William Crawford served in the post before he ran for president in 1824, a campaign that effectively denied Andrew Jackson an electoral college majority that year. Ironically, John Tyler was the president pro tempore prior to his election as vice president and his ascendancy to the presidency where he served without either a vice president or for a considerable time without a president pro tempore.

William King of Alabama was in the position before his election as vice president under Pierce. His death at the start of Pierce's term meant that this great president also had to serve much of his term without any successor available if he became unable (perhaps through his drinking bouts) to do the duties of the presidency. David Atchinson of Missouri served as president pro tempore, and perhaps by holding the post was also the de jure (if not de facto) acting president on March 4, 1849. The day was a Sunday, and both Zachary Taylor and Millard Filmore refused to take their oaths of office on a Sunday, the day that the term of James Polk ended. It is rumored that Atchinson a hearty "party man" had tied a good one on that Saturday night, and after coming to his boarding house fell fast and deep asleep—awaking on Monday morning. A good way to spend a presidency.

Benjamin Wade of Ohio was President Pro Tempore at the time of the impeachment trial of Andrew Johnson. Had an impeachment conviction been rendered in the senate (it lost by a single vote), Wade would have become president. Wade voted for conviction. Senator David Davis was an independent. However, he made his fame by an act of political dexterity. In 1877 he resigned from a seat on the U.S.Supreme Court to avoid being made the tie breaking representative of a special commission to rule on the legitimacy of electoral votes in the 1876 election between Samuel Tilden and Rutherford Hayes. His resignation was accompanied by his selection to be a U.S. Senator by the Illinois legislature. Five years later he was president pro tempore of the senate.

The Interlude of Unimportance

After the death of Cleveland's vice president, a change in succession was set into place by an act in 1886. Sentiment held that the line of succession should be of same party as president, and also executive experience as rendered with cabinet experience would be valuable for anyone assuming duties of presidency. The line of succession went to cabinet offices as then existing starting with state, treasury, war and justice, and following in order of office creations.

Nineteen Senators served as president pro tempore until 1947 under this arrangement, with the office being out of the line of succession. Most were little remembered senators. In their numbers were Isham Harrison of Tennessee, George Moses of New Hampshire, Pat Harrison of Mississippi, and Key Pittman of Nevada. Nevadans of course remember (rather—try to forget) Pittman, an alcoholic who not only held from 1933 to 1941 the then almost meaningless (thank God) position of president pro tempore, but also the very very important post as chair of the foreign relations committee. On more than one occasion he showed up at a meeting with President Roosevelt and foreign high dignitaries completely and obviously plastered. The interregnum of unimportance also included moments of service by Senator Henry Cabot Lodge and future vice president Charles Curtis. Curtis, a Republican (emphasis to be made explicit) has been the only minority (Native American) to have held so high a post in our government.

Power Restored—The Latter Years.

Notwithstanding the record of his senate colleague Key Pittman, President Truman wanted the post of president pro tempore back on the succession list.

Within a month of Harry Truman's rise to the presidency, he expressed the belief that no person holding the duties of the presidency should do so unless he (or she) had been first subject to the electoral process. He thought that members of congress fit that bill, but cabinet members did not. He felt it would be embarrassing to have a president (even if only an acting president) who has been personally selected by the president (e.g., a cabinet member). He urged a new succession line. He recommended that the line go—after vice president—to speaker of house then president pro tempore. He wished also that a new election for president be held quickly.

The speaker at the time was the very popular Sam Rayburn. The House quickly passed a bill including his basic recommendation. (They did leave out his recommendation that a special election for a new president be called immediately after such a succession). The senate, perhaps taken aback by the fact that their presiding officer was now placed behind the house speaker, balked. When Senator James Byrnes of South Carolina became secretary of state, they delayed further. However, in 1946, the Republicans secured majorities in both houses of congress and the plan seemed to be politically acceptable to both houses, as succession would go next to a republican rather than a Democrat of Truman's choosing. Truman signed the new succession act in 1947. It provided that after vice president, speaker of the house, and president pro tempore came the cabinet offices in order that they were created, the first being the secretary of state.

With the essential power of the post restored—its status of being "but three hearts beats away" from the White House, the position fell into the hands of Senator Arthur Vandenberg of Michigan. The Republicans must today feel a sense of honor at having selected a giant to the post. Vandenberg served hand in hand with Roosevelt and Truman as the minority leader of the foreign relations committee in the senate. In stark contrast to the drunken Pittman, Michigan's Vandenberg performed admirable service to the nation as the architect of bipartisanship in foreign policy at a most critical time in our history. He became the epitome of the remark that "Politics stops at the water's edge." (Contrast his role to that of President Pro Tempore Henry Cabot Lodge vis-a-vis Woodrow Wilson).

The list of the president pro tempores since the 1947 act, however, belies the notion that true leadership or moral leadership was ever again to be a prerequisite for securing the position.

Examine the following list:

Arthur Vandenberg R, MI   1947-1949
Kenneth McKellar D. TN   1949-1953
Styles Bridges R, NH   1953-1955
Walter George D, GA   1956-1957
Carl Hayden D, AZ   1957-1969
Richard Russell D, GA   1969-1971
Allen Ellender D, LA   1971-1972
James Eastland D, MI   1972-1978
Warren Magnuson D, WA   1979-1980, 1980-1981
Milton Young R, ND   1980 (One Day)
Strom Thurmond R, SC   1981-1987, 1995-2001
John Stennis D, MS   1987-1989
Robert Byrd D, WV   1989-1995, 2001

While before the ascendancy of Strom Thurmond the Republicans at least put senators of stature and national acceptability in the position, the same, with an exception or two, cannot be said of the Democrats—including their great liberal base—ergo Lyndon Johnson, Edward (Ted) Kennedy, Hubert Humphrey, George Mc Govern....

They did pick Carl Hayden, albeit at a time that he was a very very old (OK not ancient, like Thurmond or Byrd) man, and they did pick Warren Magnuson for a short time as he was aging.

The other Democrats have all been persons from rank segregationist origins, and it might be suggested, segregationists at the time of their service. I will give Byrd a benefit of the doubt (something Democrats won't give to Republicans), his Ku Klux Klan service seems to be behind him—but how far behind. (Come to think of it Democrats are never bothered that their great president Harry Truman joined and then retracted his membership in the Klan, because he found the Klan had prejudices against Jewish people, and he had a Jewish business partner. I assume Truman knew of the bigotry the Klan had against AFRICAN AMERICANS). Albeit the case, the likes of Senators George, Russell, Ellender, Eastland, and Stennis must leave an indelible mark on the liberal leaders of the Democrat party today. I believe a freudian concept is in play re the Lott imbroglio. It is called "projection."

The case of the one day term of Milton Young brings some questions regarding integrity to mind. It was his last day in the senate, so it was felt he should have a special honor. He had been in the senate since 1945, some honor was certainly due. But it was such a stupid idea to honor a very old person when his service to the land is about to end with a post that would make him president in case of a tragedy such as occurred on 9-11. How stupid can our senate be? But there was also probably some method in the madness. Was the one day appointment a pension salary grab? The president pro tempore does receive a higher salary than other senators. Maybe the senators received their pensions based upon "last salary." If so, the move would have been a blatant fraud on the American public. Hopefully, it wasn't.

Wither 2003.

Lott had to go for reasons of effectiveness. He wears the sign of Cain, and he just ain't Able. He can't lead. But the majority leadership post is not the issue. In this day of world terrorism—a terrorism that targets the United States, we must have in the line of succession persons capable of becoming president and acting as need be. The current vice president has held a high cabinet position, and he has political visibility, he could serve. Dennis Hastert has demonstrated a measure of leadership that might suffice, in a pinch. Thurmond and Byrd would be out of the picture, and thank God, they now are out of the picture.

The Republicans in Senate must not now simply give the post to someone that is on some automatic list of deserving for past service, or length of service. My first choices are Elizabeth Dole and

John McCain. Dole because among the senators (along with Warren) she has most extensive executive (cabinet and Red Cross) service, and also she put forth a national candidacy. Mc Cain among all the Republican senators put forth the most credible national campaign. But then the Republicans would really be doing the Nation a great service if they chose the one who would be most acceptable if it ever came to secession—Senator Joseph Lieberman.

Another idea or two—maybe the Republican Senate could play the "political card." They do not have to place a Senator into the post of president pro tempore. That is not a constitutional requirement. They could select J. C. Watts. And my final idea—Congress should just pass a law taking the president pro tempore of the senate off the list of posts in the line of succession to the Presidency.

HNN, January 6, 2003

William N. Thompson

4. I Got My Job Because of Affirmative Action—And I Was a 40 Year Old White Male

The words "Affirmative Action" conjure up many notions in the minds of advantaged groups in our society: "reverse discrimination," "quotas," "hiring unqualified minorities," and other such thoughts. Perhaps white male students in college today feel that "Affirmative Action" programs adopted by both private and public employers place them at a severe disadvantage in the job marketplace when they graduate. In the following case study you are asked to consider both advantages and disadvantages of the concept of affirmative action to different groups of job applicants today. Are the students better off or worse off than before there were such programs? Just why are some people so quick to condemn the notions of affirmative action? Can a common ground be found for analyzing the issue? Can there be a single "public interest" served by affirmative action policies? Can policies be viewed as a unifying "positive sum" game, benefiting the entire society, or must affirmative action always be played as a divisive "zero sum" game, only benefiting some at a direct cost to others?

This is how I got my job.

I received my undergraduate and master's degrees in political science from Michigan State University. Following a brief stint in the Marine Corps and a two year teaching position at Southeast Missouri State College in Cape Girardeau, I enrolled in the Ph.D. program at the University of Missouri in Columbia. I received my degree in 1972, nine months after I entered the job market for a tenure-track teaching position. I knew that finding a job in 1971 would not be easy. After all, my degrees were not from Ivy League schools, or from what would generally be considered "Top Ten" institutions—although the colleges were certainly respectable second line schools. Moreover, my final degree had not yet been awarded. I had an added disadvantage in the fact that I was physically located a thousand miles away from my university. I was working with a non-profit government research group in Raleigh, North Carolina.

I needed help, so I called my advisor in Missouri and asked him if he knew of any positions. He told me he didn't, but he added that I should contact a very close friend of his who was on the faculty at the University of North Carolina, which is located in Chapel Hill, only 20 miles from Raleigh. I certainly agreed that a short drive was worth the try. His friend had been a close colleague while they were both Ph.D. students at the University of Michigan in the fifties. His friend had also been on the faculty at the University of Iowa in the sixties. The North Carolina professor indicated that he really couldn't help me, but I was free to look through their departmental file of job listings if I wished to. I certainly wished to, and I did.

I found four or five items of interest. One was a penciled note on a three by five inch piece of note pad paper from a Western Michigan University professor. The professor had been a Ph.D. student of the North Carolina professor while the latter was at Iowa. The note had a personal salutation followed by a request for a new Ph.D. or near-Ph.D with an interest in public administration and an emphasis in organization theory. While the area of interest wasn't exactly what I had in mind—my degree was in political science with an emphasis in state and local government, I thought it might be worth a try. My dissertation was focused on the office of state attorney general, and that was an administrative position, sort of anyway.

Besides, I remembered the name of the Western Michigan professor from a seminar I had attended two years previously. I had met the professor and was pretty sure he would remember me. I made a personal contact, and I was informed to get to the Midwest Political Science Conference being held the next month in Chicago. There I could meet other Western faculty members. A bigger trip, but this was a tenure-track job I was seeking. The meeting in Chicago went well, and I was invited to Kalamazoo a few days later. There I was impressed that the faculty desired me to make a presentation on my dissertation research, and they seemed genuinely interested in my graduate studies. A week later I had a job offer.

I was at Western Michigan for nine years. I recall several more trips to political science conferences in Chicago. Once I drove over with the department chair and another senior professor. They talked about the new recruit we had to find for our program. Several times the two men groaned about having to post the listing and sit in a hotel room talking all day with potential candidates, and then having to respond to telephone calls that could go on until three in the morning. They let me know it was easier for them when they knew that I was coming to Chicago two years before, and that they didn't have to go through a "meat market" recruiting effort. I had been the last person the department had hired. When we got to Chicago, it turned out that they had "lucked out" again. They met a former colleague for breakfast. He told them that a fine person had been recommended by a friend at a university in Wisconsin. The candidate, it turned out, had found the atmosphere for his research at the university to be rather undesirable, and he wished another placement. The former colleague assured the chair and the senior faculty member that the candidate was top-notch, and besides, "he had his degree in hand from an eastern university." The chair quickly made a call leaving a message for the candidate, and then he called the placement service for the conference and had the Western Michigan job listing removed. The Political Science Department had its "new man." He was offered a contract two weeks later.

During my nine years at Western Michigan University, I had received tenure and been promoted to associate professor. Nonetheless, I felt that my career was in a period of stagnation. I had served a year as a National Association of Schools of Public Administration and Affairs (NASPAA) Fellow with the Labor Department in Washington, and I had been elected to a political post as the head of a local government in suburban Kalamazoo. It was 1980, and I was looking for something different. I could run for reelection and cut all ties with Western Michigan University if I won—not a sure thing, but I had a good chance. Of course, if I did that my career would be tied to electoral politics for years to come, not an overly happy prospect, from my academic perspective.

But I didn't want to return to full time teaching duties at Western as the university was facing all sorts of budget cuts and various other factors of malaise. So one day I got a copy of the Public Administration Times, the official publication of the American Society for Public Administration (ASPA). There were about a dozen jobs listed for which I was qualified. I wrote to ten of the schools and sent them my resume. One of the schools was the University of Nevada, Las Vegas. Their job announcement indicated that they desired to have a person at a mid-career rank, and that they were an "Equal Opportunity Employer." The rest is history, I got the job. There had been 32 applicants, I was ranked second, and I was invited for an interview after their first ranked candidate did not pass muster.

I have been at the University of Nevada, Las Vegas for over 20 years. My career has taken rather new twist as I have dedicated my research efforts to intensive studies of public policy and the legalized gambling industry. I can say unequivocally that I got my job at UNLV because of Affirmative Action. I was white, I was male, I was forty years old—I was an affirmative action hire.

I did not know anyone at UNLV when I was hired. No one with the Public Administration Department at UNLV knew anyone at the University of Missouri or Western Michigan University. I had no connections. However affirmative action requirements demanded that UNLV not recruit a new professor via pencilled notes, breakfast meetings, or telephone calls to insiders. They had to advertise the job. They had to advertise nationally in publications that would reach all potential job candidates. They had to make a special effort to advertise in media that would be seen by minority candidates, but they had to advertise in any job listing service for the discipline of Public Administration. They advertised with the American Political Science Association and with ASPA.

Does affirmative action help white males of younger or middle ages. This professor thinks so. In 1971 I would never have been hired by UNLV. I wonder about the "old boys" network that was in place then in Las Vegas. It does seem that many of our older professors have degrees from the Universities of Arkansas and Arizona, while several have degrees from a variety of California schools. Very few of these professors have told me that they had to compete for their positions. In 1980 I had a chance. How about the others that had a chance in 1980 that would not have had a chance in 1971? Were most of them minorities or women? I doubt it. Most Ph.D.s competing for academic jobs are males, and most are white. Without affirmative action rules, they would be left out of consideration. They would not have the simple opportunity to apply for the jobs. I was at the right place at the right time in 1971. I got a job because I could apply. While I can tell myself that I won the position because I was the best person to apply, I know the truth. I think I was qualified for the job, but I happened to have an advisor who had a good friend who happened to have a former student at a certain university who was willing to tell him about the opening. And I just happened to have met the former student at a seminar. Affirmative action means that all potential candidates know about the opening. And that means that white males have the best chances, because after all, there just happens to be a lot of them, and a lot of them do not have special connections.

HNN, June 25, 2001

5. The Biggest Affirmative Action Program of All

On June 25 (2001), I suggested that affirmative action was responsible for my securing an academic job in 1980. I am from the majority race, of the male gender, and I was 40 years old at the time. I found affirmative action to give great advantages to white males. Quite simply we are the leading category of job seekers, and affirmative action requires that jobs be widely advertised so everyone can find out about them. If everyone does, that means more white males than any other group finds out about them. More white males apply, more white males get the jobs. Still, I am not sure that the argument is persuasive for many who feel they have been "victimized" by affirmative action. And these many do include white males.

Affirmative action is not a new program for groups of government job seekers. It has been around in one form or another for over two centuries. In other incarnations affirmative action has been an accepted policy, one that was on the political agenda until it was established and then quickly off as no one seemed to challenge it. It was not a contentious issue, and it won very wide support in society. Perhaps if we can look at the dimensions of an affirmative action program that did have near universal acceptance, we can design new programs with the same qualities and the same political results—that is acceptance and willing compliance.

The program of hiring preferences for Native Americans in the Bureau of Indian Affairs has been widely accepted, but let's look at the biggest affirmative action program of all—veteran's preference. Veteran's preference was practiced in very limited ways as early as the George Washington presidential administration—and probably earlier in the days of the Articles of Confederation. Washington established a firm principle in his hiring practices that left preferences for those who served with him during the Revolutionary War unchallenged. Only qualified persons would be selected for government jobs. If a veteran was not qualified to do the job (notice the concept of job validity came early into the system), a qualified non-veteran would be given the job.

Veteran's preference programs were formalized after the Civil War and again after World War I and II. In 1889 the notion of extra points on examination scores was introduced. In 1919 veterans were moved to the top of hiring lists if they passed examinations. In 1923 President Warren Harding distinguished between veterans and disabled veterans giving extra preference to the latter group. Our present system is based upon 1944 legislation. As revised, the program keeps Washington's key point—no preference unless the job candidate is qualified. Only veterans having passing scores on exams won preference points. The preference points given were exact. A veteran was given five additional points to his/her passing score—which had to be at least 70 on a 100 point basis.

Disabled veterans (also their spouses, as well as war widows under some conditions) were given ten points, and placed into a separate group from which hires had to be made as long as persons were in the group. Under pressure from women's groups, the program was restricted to persons of major rank or less, and limited in use for promotions, and also limited for a number of years after the veteran left the service.

The program worked and works today because only qualified people are hired under its rules, and more importantly, because its rules are open, known by all, and applied in an exact manner without ambiguity. It is also tied to a policy of helping deserving persons.

Thomas Jefferson enunciated the concept that the bureaucracy—government job holders—should "represent" the public they served. His thoughts were that if the society at large was 50% Democrat and 50% Republican, the parties should have the same 50-50 representation among job holders. When Coleman Young became mayor of Detroit, he enunciated exactly the same policy for city employees—except his focus of representation was on the racial composition of the population.

In contrast to veterans preference programs, affirmative action—while helping the masses by requiring open advertising of all jobs—falls very short on honesty and openness, and on its simplicity and understandability for the general public. It uses quotas, but quotas are never used. It is overt discrimination, but it is called everything else.

Veterans preference is overt discrimination and it is not denied. The ambiguous inexact quality of affirmative action turns it into a meaningless exercise in bothersome paper work in some agencies, and a rigid abusive form of bigotry in the hands of other agencies. Each agency seems to come up with its own approach. At our university the vice president can make "opportunity hires" from selected groups whenever he wishes without any strict guidelines. For regular hires, all departments go through the paperwork nightmare of counting just how many of what group applied for each job. The "group" membership is defined by the job applicant—no D.N.A. testing. A white spouse with an Hispanic name qualifies sometimes, doesn't some other times. One judge orders that an agency must hire one African American for each white person hired in some endless future; another judge mandates targets. No exact rules. No certain policy. This invites cynicism, this hinders policy acceptance. Moreover, there is no enunciation of a public policy goal in the programs.

To make affirmative action acceptable, exact rules for its operations should be put into place. We should recognize that there is a realistic merit in the concepts advanced by Thomas Jefferson and Coleman Young—bureaucrats do represent those they serve. There is a validity in the notion that the type of service given and received from many bureaucrats can be affected by personal attributes of the civil servant. Discrimination is rampant in many ways in government service, a limited controlled policy that involves some new discrimination for specific policy goals should not be difficult to accept.

William N. Thompson

All affirmative action programs should utilize the ideas of George Washington and the 1944 Veterans Preference Act as revised. Only the qualified should be hired. First they must pass the test. How many preference points should they then be given? Five (on a 100 point test) for agencies where the group in question has less than half the representation that they have in the population represented (or served) by the agency. If the group is not represented at all, or critically under represented, qualified applicants could receive ten points. As soon as the agency achieved a condition of representativeness, the points would no longer be used in hiring.

Top preference should be given to ALL basic racial ethnic groups (African American, White, Asian American, Native American) as well as males and females, and the handicapped. No other groupings should be considered. There would be devils in the details, of course, but vague ambiguous conditions that exist today might be lessened to such a degree that affirmative action could become a widely accepted and non-contentious policy of governments.

HNN, July 24, 2001

6. We Are Not Victims

The concept of six degrees of separation has been on my mind since September 11. We simply were not that far away from the people in the towers. I live physically 2000 miles away, yet I connect to victims through individuals I personally know in at least three separate directions, and that means everyone I know connects through me, ergo, through at most two persons. Unlike any war before, I have visited and revisited the battle scene on the ground through television. Never before have I encountered such impediments to my travel plans. Even the quest for purchasing a round trip ticket to Los Angeles, an hour-fifteen minute flight, now has me in a quandary—can I carry-on all I need, what can I carry-on, how long will I have to wait at the airport, in Las Vegas, in Los Angeles, will the flight be on time? What trouble will I face as I wish to use the flight to connect to an international flight? I finished writing a book on my favorite subject—gambling—yet I am not enthused about promoting it. I wonder, is my publisher? When a professor finishes a book, he is supposed to celebrate. It seems so unimportant a thing today. And my city, Las Vegas, appears to have been severely affected by the national tragedy as we depend heavily upon air traffic to bring us the people that purchase our recreational and entertainment "products." Fifteen thousand in the casino industry were put out of work. Some are my students.

A S.W.O.T. Assessment

We're all affected as never before, but are we all victims? Can we possibly apply a S.W.O.T. (Strengths, Weaknesses, Opportunities, Threats) analysis to what has happened? Dare we try? We've witnessed our weaknesses, and we felt the threat, and we feel the threats. Can there possibly be strengths and opportunities coming out of September 11?

We appear to be showing resolve, yet I am very unsure about our resolve. A few years ago a member of a neo-Nazi group was captured in Las Vegas. He had come here with a test tube full of Bubonic plague and materials that were to be used for processing Anthrax. He evidently thought he had access to a medical lab in Las Vegas where he could put together materials in a way that they could be disseminated. After he was captured, the F.B.I. found tapes of him giving talks about delivering the materials to gatherings of Jews and Blacks for the purpose of accomplishing mass murder. He was a science professor. He was on probation for other crimes. He was captured. He was released.

It appears we didn't have "proof" of something or another, and that anyone could get Bubonic plague materials, so what the hell, he was just anybody. His probation was not revoked. He walked. Maybe he still walks—in Florida. I hear that we may not have "evidence beyond a reasonable doubt" to convict anyone of anything—like "nothing" happened. If we have to take the World Trade Towers case to an "O.J." jury, I seriously question our resolve. I doubt if we could "convict" the 22 "most-wanted." We appear to be showing a great display of patriotism, and I suspect this is a strength right now. But I don't feel that flag waving gives us enough strength in and of itself. We do have opportunities. We are getting new geography lessons, and for years studies have show that as a nation we have been rather illiterate regarding geography and lives of other peoples. Not much, but it's something.

The Opportunity

However, one real opportunity exists. Our best opportunity may come in the national and personal reflections upon just who we are, collectively, but especially who we are as individuals. It was only that proverbial month plus days ago, that I was being besieged with calls about the $300 million dollar Powerball lottery drawing. I appeared on CNN's "Crossfire," as well as "Wolf Blitzer News" to talk about the big lotteries. I even wrote an HNN column on the subject. Funny, no one has even raised the question of lotteries lately.

I have received calls about the economy of Las Vegas, but those are serious inquiries about real people trying to sustain their livelihoods in a leisure industry town.

I have not been asked to talk about gamblers and their mindset. I think back a month plus days ago to a statement that accompanied the Powerball hoopla. One lottery commentator observed that the public was no longer interested in lotto games if the prize was to be only $40, $50, or $60 million. Such a "minuscule" prize amount was not effective for attracting masses of players, because "people wanted to know that the prize they won would be sufficient for them to completely change their lives." In other words, it appeared to be that for the masses in America, their lives "sucked," at least so much so that it would take a hundred million dollars or more to set their lives straight.

We Are Not Victims, Our Lives Have Meaning

Just a month plus days ago, as this is what I study, gambling, I pondered that observation as I watched memorial services and as I watched people in New York City walking about with pictures with names and signs, "Have You Seen This Person?" And I heard the persons carrying the signs speak. Never, Never, did they suggest that their loved one's life was meaningless or hopeless, or so devoid of content that it was not worth living sans an extra hundred million dollars.

If life was bad, it was still so much better than the alternative. But, it was not bad. I heard and the nation heard them proclaiming that life was good, that people were good. Of course, we had many new heroes to admire, but it was the ordinary people buried in an anonymous rubble of the terrorist destruction who were good and wonderful people. I pondered the awful question, "did they buy lottery tickets?" If they did, it sure seemed that those marketing the tickets had missed the mark—these people loved the lives they were leading, and they loved the people who were around them in those lives. They and those around them did not want to change their lives.

William N. Thompson

It is a simple observation, but maybe not an unimportant one. A tragedy shined the light on goodness of people in America, people in our lives, people removed from us by so few degrees of separation, and a renewed awareness of that goodness is truly one opportunity for growth that has come our way since 9-11. By seizing upon this opportunity we all may escape the trap of victimhood.

    HNN, October 5, 2001

Parables from (a not quite) Paradise, NV 89154

7. The Worst Day in American History

The recent display of Osama Bin Laden's cheer and joy is reminiscence of Adolph Hitler's little dance of happiness when he heard of his army's successes in France. It probably solidifies in many minds the notion that September 11 was the worse day in American History, and that Bin Laden is historically the arch enemy number one. I dissent partially—regarding the first point.

One of our prominent state governors of the modern era gave a press conference one day after it had been publicly revealed that his son had been arrested for theft. A crying Lester Maddox proclaimed that the worst thing in life is to confront the fact that your child has done wrong. It is tragic to lose battles, it is tragic to see American lives lost in battle, it is tragic to lose lives when our country is attacked by enemies. But perhaps the worse days of our history are the days when Americans have done wrong, or Americans have caused innocents to lose their lives.

We should not have to reflect on Oklahoma City, Sand Creek or Wounded Knee or Nagasaki in moments as today, for we must have a resolve that we can secure a safe world in an honorable way albeit a way that must involve violence, a justified use of violence. We shouldn't have to rank order absurdities of the human condition either, yet we are asked to at times.

Hence I will discuss my candidate for the worse day in American History, and I will discuss a culprit that was well meaning, passive, a victim of circumstances, but nonetheless a culprit.

My day of infamy is April 19, 1784. My American culprit of all time was Congressman John Beatty.

In 1784 the Article of Confederation congress met in Annapolis. Delegates to congress were selected by the 13 states. Each state could send from two to seven delegates, and the delegates would collectively cast the state's single vote on each issue. The Articles required that two delegates be present from a state for the state to participate in any vote. Seven affirmative votes were necessary for a measure to pass.

With all of his other foibles, Congressman Thomas Jefferson recognized that the institution of slavery was a curse in our nation. Slavery was antithetical to the words he carved in stone in our Declaration of Independence. It was contrary to the essence of our American Dream. It was instead a nightmare that made any "dream" but an illusion.

Jefferson hesitated to hit slavery head on, but he truly wished that slavery would not spread across our soil. In early 1784 he proposed legislation that outlined a pattern for development of unsettled western lands. The pattern included a framework for new governments and also a bill of rights that included a measure to prohibit slavery. All the western lands, then collectively controlled by the national government, would be free lands. The lands that in the near future would become Ohio, Indiana, Illinois, Michigan, and Wisconsin (and part of Minnesota), as well as Kentucky, Tennessee, Florida, Alabama, and parts of Louisiana and Georgia would forever be free lands.

Had the proposal only passed! Slavery—to any large extent—would have been contained to the south Atlantic states. With that containment, an abolition movement could have proceeded with a growing national consensus, and could been accomplished with out the bitter taste of violence that remains on our collective national psyche—not soon enough by any means, but sooner than the Missouri Compromise, "Bleeding Kansas," Harper's Ferry, and the Civil War.

Bin Laden and Hitler could not have danced in greater joy than they would have danced had they seen our nation engrossed in that bloody struggle of American against American.

The story of April 19, 1784. The debate led to a separate vote on the question of abolishing and prohibiting slavery in all the western lands. The votes were tallied: New Hampshire, two in favor. Massachusetts, two in favor. Rhode Island, two in favor. Pennsylvania, three in favor. Connecticut, two in favor. New York, two in favor. Six state votes in favor.

South Carolina, two votes against. Maryland, two votes against. Virginia, Mr. Jefferson votes in favor, his two fellow delegates vote against. Three states vote against.

North Carolina votes one in favor, one against. No state vote recorded. Delaware is absent. Georgia is absent. New Jersey's delegate, Samuel Dick, votes in favor; the state's second delegate is absent. The votes of these states do not count.

The tally: 16 delegates vote in favor, seven vote against. Six votes cast by states are in favor. Three votes cast by states are against. The measure fails.

The measure fails quite simply because New Jersey's second delegate is absent. His name was John Beatty.

John Beatty was born in 1749 in Neshaminy, Bucks County, Pennsylvania. He was the son of the Reverend Charles Beatty, an early trustee of the College of New Jersey (now Princeton University), where John Beatty graduated in 1769. John was a patriot being commissioned in 1776 in the Pennsylvania Battalion. On November 16, 1776 while fighting with Washington's main force in New York, Beatty and 2817 other patriot men in arms were captured by the British. He was exchanged for British prisoners and given freedom in May 1778.

He knew the horrors of captivity. It was a brutal experience as he was often beaten by his British captors. Beatty was then given the rank of colonel and appointed commissary-general of all war prisoners. He resigned from the Army in 1780 amidst charges that he had violated rules by trading with the enemy.

He returned to Trenton, New Jersey, where he became engaged in professional and business life, and where he entered politics. He oversaw the building of the first bridge over the Delaware River, and he organized the first bank in Trenton. He was very involved in church work serving as a trustee of the Trenton Presbyterian Church. He was appointed to a term in congress from 1783 to 1785. Afterwards he was a delegate to the New Jersey convention that ratified the Constitution, and he served in the New Jersey Assembly for several terms, one as speaker, and in 1793 he returned to the national congress. Beatty died in 1826 and his remains are in the cemetery beside the Presbyterian Church on the Trenton Mall.

A leading life as a local notable, but in national terms a rather ordinary political life, except for the events of the Spring of 1784. His letters in the Library of Congress include one addressed to Governor Livingstone urging that New Jersey send a second delegate to Annapolis quickly, as he was "clearly of the opinion" that his fellow members were ignoring his arguments as they could not be backed by a vote. When Samuel Dick arrived in Annapolis, Beatty wrote that they got along well and agreed in all matters of "politicks and religion."

Beatty was not a violent monster. (*But see below, Essay 7a). In a reverse of Woody Allen's observation that 80% of life is "showing up," for Beatty 100% of his crime was simply not showing up. He was in Annapolis, but where? He was at his rooming house. He was sick in bed. While he was involved in many business ventures, John Beatty's primary profession was medicine. The physician was sick in bed, the physician could not heal himself, and the physician could not render one vote that could have helped healed our nation of its most mortal wound, the wound that keeps bleeding, slavery.

HNN, December 17, 2001

7a. John Beatty: "And Now for the Rest of the Story." Maybe.

I have been telling the story about John Beatty and the "Worst Day in American History" for well over 25 years. When I was a Public Administration Fellow in Washington, D.C., in 1977, I ventured to the Library of Congress and discovered his letters, and I read them. I also visited Ken and Dee Tillman, good friends in Trenton, New Jersey, and we trekked to the city mall and paid our respects at Beatty's gravestone. I had accepted the story that Beatty had been home "sick in bed" on April 19, 1784, and I had without question accepted that his vote would have been with Jefferson's proposal. His colleague Samuel Dick voted to ban slavery, and he had written that he and Dick agreed in all matters of "politicks." However, an email I received on June 7, 2003, now raises potential doubts upon my assumptions. While I do not retreat from my position that the event and the day were the "worst" in our history—and maybe I am even more firm in that belief as a result of the email—I am questioning whether perhaps I should to revise my assumptions regarding Beatty. Maybe he was not sick at all. Maybe his views were proslavery. Of even worse, maybe he was "bribed" to stay away so that the pro-slavery forces could have that day—and we could have our "little" war some three score and seventeen years later.

The email was sent by Dr. Bill Luken who took it upon himself to dig into some family histories of personal interest. Dr. Luken is a scientist. He received his Ph.D. in Chemistry from the Yale University, and he has been on the faculties of Mississippi State University and Duke University. He has been working for IBM since 1985 in computer graphics and multimedia software. Dr. Luken wrote:

I recently "discovered" your column entitled "The Worst Day in Our History." I have also noticed that this issue was raised in the book <u>Understanding Thomas Jefferson,</u> by E.M. Halliday. You might be interested to learn about another event in which John Beatty was a (passive) participant.

In 1806, John Beatty was co-executor for the estate of "Hon." Joseph Reading, son of John Reading, twice acting colonial governor of New Jersey—1747 and 1757. (Luken references a web site: http://Luken.us/genealogy/JosephReadingsWilll.htm which presents Reading's will and some rather damning evidence supporting his e-mail statement).

John Reading twice served as "president of council" (aka "acting governor") in the intervals between the demise of one "real" colonial governor and the appointment of a successor. As a result, he is called "Gov. John Reading." Gov. John Reading was also one of the founders of the College of New Jersey, now known as Princeton University.

Joseph Reading was entitled to the honorific "Hon." because he had been a judge in certain courts in New Jersey. It may be that "Dishonorable" Joseph Reading might be more appropriate.

The other co-executor was Pierson Reading, grandson of "Hon." Joseph Reading by his son Joseph Reading, Jr. John Beatty was a grandson of Gov. John Reading and so a nephew to "Hon." Joseph Reading.

At the time of "Hon." Joseph Reading's death (1806), his family seemed to be split between pro-slavery and abolitionist factions. Gov. John Reading had died in 1768, so he was out of the picture. The pro-slavery faction included Hon. Joseph Reading, John Beatty, and Pierson Reading.

William Reading and Joseph Reading Jr., sons of "Hon." Joseph Reading, married sisters Ann and Lucy Emley. Ann and Lucy were daughters of Elisha Emley, and descendants of Quaker immigrant William Emley. I suspect that the Emley family were still Quakers, but I have not proven this. Quakers were generally opposed to slavery by 1800. Assuming the Emley family were either Quakers or shared Quaker-like values, William and Joseph probably espoused the abolitionist cause.

By 1806, William Reading had died, but Joseph Reading, Jr. was still living. It must have been an awful life, with both his father and son Pierson promoting slavery while he was an abolitionist. No wonder he died only a few years later. As a result, William Reading and Joseph Reading, Jr. were disinherited, and Joseph's son was treated like a son by his grandfather's will. The net result was to impoverish the abolitionist and enrich the pro-slavery faction.

About 20 years later (ca 1826), it looks like Pierson Reading and his family moved to Mississippi where he established a slave-based plantation near Vicksburg. That enriched his position even further. One of his sons was Maj. Pierson Barton Reading who moved to California in 1843 or 1844 where his exploits are legendary.

Pierson Reading died during an epidemic of yellow fever in New Orleans in 1847. His son, Maj. Pierson B. Reading, discovered gold on his property (Rancho Buena Ventura) near Shasta. He was a Whig candidate for governor of California in 1851, losing by a very narrow margin. He married Fannie Washington whose father was a nephew of President George Washington, and whose mother was a descendent of "Light Horse Harry" Lee.

Meanwhile, a typical career for a descendent of the abolitionist faction during the 1800s and early 1900s was train conductor. Some individuals fared better than others, but none was ever a state-level or national-level political figure. It is possible to conclude that the bad guys won.

As co-executor, John Beatty did not need to do anything (his strong suit?). Joseph Reading's will continues to confound his descendants because it refers to his grandson Pierson as his "son." Consequently, even the victims of this affair remain blinded by the lies of the "Hon." Joseph Reading.

As for John Beatty in April 1784, it looks to me like he must have sold his vote to pro-slavery interests. After all, he was in Annapolis, below the Mason-Dixon line. He must have been surrounded by wealthy slave-holders who would have been eager to shell out a few coins to preserve their way of life, or else burn down his house back in New Jersey if he did not get "sick."

Dr. Luken has reiterated this interpretation of events in subsequent e-mails, but I must be fair to him. He offers the views only as speculation, he does not categorically assert or confirm as "fact" that Beatty was other than "sick in bed."

Just food for thought. The corruption or malfeasance of many past administrations—Grant, Harding, Nixon—the personal foibles of Kennedy and Clinton, the questionable policy choices of Truman or Johnson, the non-activity of a Buchanan, all of these pale in significance if we could ever conclude that this one man, John Beatty, purposefully and for selfish reasons avoided the opportunity to cast a vote that could have ended slavery in our land many decades prior to the Fifteenth Amendment, and could have rendered totally unnecessary the entire Civil War.

8. St. Clair, Little Turtle, Little Crow and Little Six and Retribution

The events of September 11 are unprecedented in so many ways, yet they call out for a search for any historical parallels and lessons—perhaps unlearned, perhaps yet to be learned. The recent tragedies do not represent to first time that the United States's interests and people have been attacked on our own soil. They do not represent the first time that an adversary has inflicted massive casualties upon civilian populations.

The nature of two incidents in history and their aftermath deserve reflection: the defeat of General (and Governor) Arthur St. Clair at the hands of Little Turtle and allies of Tecumseh and Blue Jacket in 1791, and the Sioux Uprising in Minnesota in 1862.

On October 25, 1791 President George Washington proclaimed "it is sincerely to be desired that all need of coercion in the future may cease." He was talking about relationships with Native American tribes and settlers in western lands of the United States. His tone was to change in a very short time. He was soon to learn of events in Ohio.

The Shawnee Little Turtle along with Blue Jacket (a white man raised by Natives), and Tecumseh refused to recognize Ohio land deals made with white settlers—some by treaties (with other tribes), some by purchases from French and British. As a result of the imbroglio, President Washington had authorized that an expedition to protect settlers and subdue Shawnee excursions onto the lands held by the governor of the Northwest Territories, General Arthur St. Clair. St Clair had a force of 1400, mostly untrained militia. Perhaps, it is possible some were conscripts from the settlements, as the "Letters of St. Clair" specifically ask that he be allowed to draft soldiers. He placed the troops on a vulnerable plateau above the Upper Wabash River in western Ohio on the evening of November 3, 1791. The next morning using great stealth, Little Turtle attacked. His forces were trained for the fight. The U.S. military suffered it worse defeat ever on American soil (excepting the Civil War), as 623 soldiers were killed along with 24 civilian muleskinners. The wounded numbered 172. The casualties were nearly three times as great as those suffered by George Armstrong Custer at Little Big Horn in 1876.

St. Clair survived the battle, but he was replaced in command by General "Mad Anthony" Wayne in 1792. The United States government sought a peaceful conclusion to the disaster, but a treaty party was murdered by the Native Americans in 1792. In 1793 a peace meeting was held, but it only resulted in an ultimatum from Little Turtle that the settlers abandon all lands north of the Ohio—an unacceptable (and unenforceable) demand. Wayne prepared to do battle—and he knew how to prepare his armies. Congress gave its full support to his plans, and President Washington had lost his conciliatory mood. Hoping for the support of the British (who contrary to the Treaty of 1783 had not left the region), Little Turtle attacked Wayne. The result at first was a stalemate, but when the British refused to join ranks with the Shawnee and their allies, the tide turned. Wayne led a daring and decisive charge against the Native Americans at Fallen Timbers (south of present day Toledo) on August 20, 1794. This was the real end for the Native Americans in the area known as the Northwest Territories. In 1795, the Treaty of Greenville ceded all of the land in the Territories to the United States with the proviso that the tribes have reservations and that they be given food supplies in recognition of limitations on complete open access for hunting and fishing.

The treaty basically held with the exception of the activity of Tecumseh and his brother who with their peoples refused to retreat to reservations. In reaction to the threats from Tecumseh, General William Henry Harrison established himself as an American hero by decimating Tecumseh's village on the Tippecanoe River, near what is now Lafayette, Indiana. Hail to the Old Gold and Black. Harrison whose fame led him to a short term as president, chased Tecumseh into Canada, where again the Native leader thought he would have some British support. Tecumseh was killed by Harrison's army in

1812. Interestingly, the officer credited (perhaps self-credited) with firing the bullet killing Tecumseh was Richard Johnson, who used this moment of fame to win the vice presidency in 1836—if the Whigs can run the man who defeated Tecumseh for president, the Democrats will run the man who actually killed Tecumseh for vice president. The defeat of St. Clair was fully avenged. (Not "justice," but avenged).

    The Greenville Treaty led to a pattern of reservations and promises of food and supplies. As settlers moved to areas near the Native reserves, they expected that there would be peaceful coexistence. This did occur in many places. However, in June 1862, the Sioux in Minnesota were experiencing food shortages. The Indian Agents of the U.S. Government who were known to be corrupt, refused to distribute provisions. The Sioux on the brink of starvation begged, but thieving agents had already stolen many of the provisions. When a person manning a storehouse suggested to the Native peoples that they could "eat the grass," it was too much. Some young Sioux killed the storehouse attendant and raided the supplies. Others then killed local merchants in town. When the word reached Little Crow, he was very hurt. He had always hoped for good relationships with the settlers. He knew that a line had been crossed and that the Army would hold the full tribe responsible for the killings. He acquiesced in the violence, and soon there were more raids and a general uprising of the Sioux against the American settlers. About 1000 civilians were killed. The U.S. Army reacted expectedly, although the demands of the Civil War tugged at them as well. A force near the "cities" was brought together and sent westward to subdue Little Crow. Little Crow arranged an ambush, but it was not effective. On September 23, 1862, Colonel Henry Sibley's forces fought off Little Crow, and the tribal army disbanded. Sibley called for them to surrender and three days later Little Crow considered that he had no option. The tribe released 370 settlers they were holding, and 2000 surrendered. It was not a happy ending, as a military tribunal condemned 303 to death, and 1700 to prison. President Lincoln was asked to intervene, and he commuted many of the death sentences. Nonetheless, 38 were hanged in the largest mass group execution in history. One was Little Six who many agree was not involved in the uprising in any violent manner. Other Sioux were rounded up and expelled from the state, being sent into the Dakotas to places like Pine Ridge and Wounded Knee. Their they had another uprising that resulted in massive losses of land after they had engaged and defeated General Custer. Today the residents of the South Dakota Sioux reservations are the poorest communities in America. In retribution for their attacks, the Sioux were essentially destroyed as a strong culture and as a viable self sufficient people. They persist in poverty—well, most do.

A remnant group of the Sioux hid during the time of the round-up and expulsion. In the Twentieth Century they won recognition as a tribe and were given a reservation in Shakopee, Minnesota, a Twin Cities suburb. The Mdewkanton Santee Sioux number but a few hundred, but they claim to be a sovereign nation. Until very recently they had been very poor people, then "bingo." Or, should the word be "jackpot." They were permitted to have a casino—the only casino in a metropolitan area of three million people—a market "to salivate for." The casino wins over one half billion dollars a year. Each tribal member receives a cash bonus in excess of $800,000 a year. Justice! Maybe not. I would certainly recognize that casinos are a good way for taking some Native peoples out of poverty—a positive thing. But, unfortunately, we have here a "new" nation of 200 or so people who seem not to be related to thousands of the poorest people in the Dakotas, with whom they feel no obligation to share their wealth. Hey, I'm a white man, I wouldn't share my wealth would I? Except I do pay my income taxes. Moreover, my culture did not have the "potlatch," a ceremony of giving to the poorer people in my community—actually, though we do have a religious value structure not at all alien to the potlatch. The casino is but one more vehicle that may be used to break the true spirit and the value structure of the Sioux people. Perhaps the Mdewkanton Santee are the ultimate victims of the retribution dispensed to people who attack American.

Lessons. Retribution follows attacks on America. Little Turtle and Little Crow each showed his "hole" card. In Las Vegas that is not the way to gamble. So too have the Arab Terrorists exposed their hand. If history has a lesson, they are history—and it won't be soon enough.

    HNN, September 13, 2001

9. The Olympic Circles in Jerusalem

Dateline Israel, Late July 2001.

1. Some Background.

1968. Mexico City. East Bloc judges witness American basketball victory, but turn back clock. In extra time awarded, Soviets score and the victory is reversed. African American athletes win Gold, then use victory platform as personal platform to protest civil rights situation in U.S.

1972. Munich. Arab World terrorists invade the Olympic Village and murder members of Israeli weightlifting team. The murderers are given sanctuary in Libya.

1980 Moscow. President Jimmy Carter mandates that U. S. athletes will not attend games in Moscow as the Soviet military has intervened in Afghanistan. Carter pressures American allies to also boycott games and many do so.

1984 Los Angeles. The Soviet Union boycotts Olympics held in Los Angeles claiming that there will not be adequate personal security for athletes. Most East Bloc countries support boycott but some do not. China sends a team to games and Chinese athletes are wildly cheered by American audiences.

2001. July 14. Moscow. Meeting in Moscow, the International Olympic Committee awards the 2008 games to Beijing, although there are openly expressed concerns over a lack of human rights in China. Within a week of the selection, American Chinese academics are arrested in China on nebulous charges of spying. They are soon released in preparation for visit by U.S. secretary of state.

2001. July 15. Jerusalem. The 16th Maccabiah Games are opened in Jerusalem amidst calls for boycotts and political protests.

2. Some Words about the 16th Maccabiah Games: A Post-Script for Moscow 1980 or a Prelude to Beijing 2008.

Our plane landed in the early afternoon on July 12. The large greeting sign at the Ben Gurion Airport near Tel Aviv proclaimed welcome to the athletes of the 16th Maccabiah Games. We looked about us as we lined up for the passport and customs check. We found we were surrounded by young people laughing and speaking Russian. Their satchels and dress clearly indicated that they were among the hundreds of Jewish athletes from throughout the world coming to compete in the games. The Maccabiah Games had been held with a few exceptions each four years since 1931. This year the games were not an occasion of unqualified celebration. Much political attention and tension surrounded the competition. The United States Maccabiah Committee had urged that the games be postponed. Then when they were not, the committee urged that U.S. athletes not compete. The American basketball coach withdrew as did several of the members of the team. However, after the committee relented and indicated it was all right for Americans to participate, a new coach was found and he quickly put together a team. The American softball team did withdraw, and the softball competition was saved at the last moment when a Venezuelan team entered (competition demanded at least three teams).

Many nations refused to allow their athletes to come. Holland boycotted the games, but a single Dutch athlete attended in defiance of his home country's committee. The Australians threatened a boycott that was withdrawn at the last moment, and the Green Party urged that all athletes, even those who made the trip to Israel, refuse to play in the games. Many teams were put together when it was agreed that expatriates living in Israel could perform as members of teams from their former countries.

The 16th games were held.

The Maccabiah Games were first held in 1931 in Tel Aviv in order to bring together Jewish athletes from throughout the world for competition in Israel. Maccabees sports organizations were first formed at the end of the Nineteenth Century in Constantinople. The organization came to Jaffa, (now) Israel, in 1906. The organization grew to 120 chapters in Israel and in almost all of the countries of the Diaspora. The games have had a message with political overtones since their inception.

The games are named for Judea of Maccabee, the hero of the Jewish people who led an outnumbered army from camps in Modi'in on a triumphal march to reclaim Jerusalem and the Second Temple from the Greeks in 164 BCE. There they cleaned the Temple and removed the icons of worship to Zeus and other Greek Gods. Then when they finished and they wished to have a long celebration, they discovered they only had oil to light their lamps for one evening. But they were destined to celebrate as the oil supply for one evening kept the lamps lighted for eight evenings of celebration. This miracle of (C)hanakuh is celebrated annually.

The message of the games was at the same time several messages—a message of international solidarity among the Jewish People of their restored homeland and the people of the Diaspora, the people who had moved to the ends of the Earth. But also it was a message of Zionism, a message of the Aliyah—the call to come home. Shortly after the first games, the athletes from Lithuania announced that they would remain in Tel Aviv, and they mailed their flag back to their home country. In 1935 the games were held under the emerging and growing shadow of Nazism. This time athletes from many European countries chose not to return home.

The tragedy of war and Holocaust and the political turmoil and war accompanying independence for Israel saw the games abandoned until 1950. With the renewal of the games in the mid-century, many of the world's top athletes have participated including Olympic gold medalists Mark Spitz, Isaac Berger, and Ron Ashworth as well as Wimbledon Tennis champion Dick Savit.

Born in an atmosphere of politics, the games remain immersed in political squabbles and international controversy.

The ostensible reason for much of the reluctance of national groups to send athletes to the 16th games in Jerusalem involves concern for their safety. It is not only irony, but it is a double punishment for Israel to see their games boycotted because of concerns for athlete safety, because it was their national weightlifting team that was sought out by the Arab terrorists and murdered in Munich in 1972. Now the terrorists seem to have again come forth to intervene in their athletic endeavors. Now the violence comes out of the Intifada, the struggle of Palestine Arabs against Israeli military and civilians usually near the lands of the Palestine Authority but also deep within uncontested Israeli lands. But there is more to the boycotts than the Intifada.

The Australian's threatened boycott results from a tragedy of the 1997 games. Then during an opening ceremony in Tel Aviv a platform bridging a river collapsed as athletes crowded on to it. Four Australians were killed but many more were also thrown into a highly polluted river, and the toxins have afflicted them with possibly lifelong diseases. Only recently was a long-term legal struggle over financial responsibility for the consequences of the accident resolved. This was not good enough for the Greens. They have demanded that the games be stopped because the particular culprit river in Tel Aviv has not been cleansed of its toxins.

Amidst all the controversy and worry the games were held. On July 23 from our Novotel Hotel rooms the fireworks over the old city of Jerusalem burst forth the celebration of the closure of the 16th Maccabiah Games. Many kudos were given to security personnel, they had done well. They had to do well, as they intercepted potential terrorists before they could act. Amidst all the controversy concerning the Jerusalem games, CNN blasted forth the news from Moscow that Beijing has the 2008 games. The IOC vote was a political vote.

The Olympics are not International games; they are a collective exercise in nationalism. The U.S.A. protested Moscow in 1980, and the U.S.A. Maccabiah Committee found reason to protest Jerusalem in 2001. Certainly, if we wish, we can look and find reason to protest Beijing in 2008. We can hope China will improve on many fronts, but on some front it will not, if we need an excuse as Jimmy Carter felt he needed in 1980, we will find one. But if we do, and even if the excuse is a compelling one, what should the nature of our response be. Must we do as Carter did?

HNN, August 20, 2001

10. Olympics Carter, Olympics Beijing

Every country and every place has its problems. Whatever site is chosen for international games can become the site of protests. We should seriously contemplate the prospects regarding the 2008 Olympic Games in Beijing.

While China is a partner rather than an adversary on the issue of terrorism, we cannot deny that China has a whole slew of problems, many of which, even the most optimistic person cannot foresee being solved by 2007 or 2008. Here are just a few: censorship, religious intolerance and subjugation, prison labor, Tibet, political prisoners, arrests of academic scholars, aggressive threats toward Taiwan, violation of copyright protections, pirating patents, selling nuclear materials to rouge nations, environmental destruction—both with air pollution and the Yangtze dam project, lack of handicapped rights, toleration of infanticide and forced abortions, harassing spies over international waters, and maybe a few others.

When the Soviet Union was awarded the 1980 games in the early seventies as part of a deal that allowed the U.S.A. to have the games in 1984, we (and the Olympic officials) were very well aware of the Gulags and the entire picture of restrained liberty in the Soviet Union. But there was an air of detente and good feelings toward the Soviet Union, and we wished to capture a spirit of cooperation with cultural exchanges among the peoples of each country.

However, the sense of improvement in relations reached an impasse as the Soviet's invaded Afghanistan in an effort to control political activity in what it considered its sphere of influence. President Jimmy Carter saw the Olympics as a tool for protest against the Soviets. He mandated that our athletes would boycott the games and he urged other countries to ask their athletes to do the same. We boycotted, and the Soviets returned the favor. In 1984 they maintained that Los Angeles was not a safe city and their athletes might be subject to criminal attacks. They boycotted the games and asked other counties to do the same. Many East Bloc countries did so.

While we may be optimistic about future relations with China, it is not out of the realm of possibility that many of the vexing problems extant in China will persist. One would have to be the proverbial "cock-eyed optimist" to really think all the problems would be solved in a way that we truly found acceptable. There will be major things wrong in China in 2008.

We should start preparing now for that eventuality. We should openly discuss the possibilities, and we should develop policy options. Now. Not at the last moment.

In 1980, President Jimmy Carter acted with great haste and in essential isolation without counsel from key directions as he mandated that the United States would boycott the Moscow Olympics. In his heart he may have been right, but then we know that in his heart there was not always purity. In his mind he may have been consulting with Amy regarding the games, but he did not consult with the athletes who in many cases spent years or even decades preparing for their participation. He did not consult with congress although there were certainly federal policy questions involved. He did not consult with Los Angeles civic and political leaders who were to host the 1984 games—and who as a result of his decision, suffered a retaliatory boycott of their games by the Soviet Union and many East Bloc countries (a boycott our Chinese "friends" did not follow). President Carter did not consult business interests involved. Perhaps they are not supposed to run America, but they did put at risk tens and hundreds of millions of dollars preparing to televise the games, equip the games and organize transportation for the games.

Carter did not consult our allies, and yet he fully expected them to blindly follow his lonely lead in the boycott. Many did so hence imposing very high costs upon their athletes and their businesses.

Most regrettably President Carter did not consult me, for I could have given him a much better alternative for protesting the bad actions of the Soviet Union. I will share my unsought advice to President Carter, and perhaps my plan for 1980 can be used in 2008 if the need arises. On the other hand, the advice may be useful for 2004 and all subsequent Olympics, regardless of where they are held.

Now more than ever, we need a spirit of internationalism. However, the Olympic spirit of internationalism has been almost totally destroyed by an obnoxious exercise in collective nationalism each four years. Each time I see a "We're Number One" sign, or hear a "USA USA USA" chant, I feel that our national values have been betrayed. I feel sickened when our Olympic representatives resort to pressure games officials to allow NBA basketball professionals to participate just so we can avert the embarrassment of seeing some other nation with a medal in what is "our" sport. Often, when I see rude strutting athletes with my fellow citizens cheering them on and waving that one finger in the air, I start cheering for the other side, any other side. The games need to be denationalized.

Carter could have struck a blow for international good will by declaring that the team from the United States would not be taking the American flag with them to Moscow. Nor would they appear in USA uniforms, nor when victorious, would the national anthem of our country be heard. National symbolism has its place in our country—a vital place after 9-11, but still our symbols of national pride also can be out of place when we wish to be building bridges for better human relations among peoples of the whole world.

We should recognize that, on the one hand, the games would be more appealing as an occasion of sports competition if we did not have players using our national symbols as if they were logos for the Cleveland Indians or Nebraska Cornhuskers.

More importantly, by keeping the flag and our national identity at home, yet still sending competitors, and still sending our national sports (and news) media, we would have told the world that we object to the behavior of the Soviet Union in Afghanistan. Our athletes could have worn their personal uniforms sans commercial logos, and they could have been encouraged to wear arm bands of protest. Moreover, athletes and fans alike from around the world could have been encouraged to use the occasion to assert their desire for peace through picket signs and protest marches in Moscow—and on camera—worldwide.

Perhaps the residents of Moscow would have even liked to join in a protest march; many were not happy to see their sons sent off to a war that made no sense to them. In this way, Carter could have projected his desire for "human rights" out to the whole world, rather than using it as a weapon of division among nations. One might think that the Soviets (or Chinese) would stop by force the kind of demonstrations and activities I am suggesting we could have encouraged. Indeed, if it was their inclination they could have stopped the games. I don't think they would have done so, but our regrets are that we did so.

No country that has ever held the Olympics was perfect. No country that sends athletes to the games is perfect. We have competed in Hitler's Berlin, in colonial London, in a politically closed Mexico City, in a Melbourne when Australia embraced its "while only" policies. We can compete in China, we have chosen China for the International games. But we should consider that there will be ways of protesting bad behavior of the Chinese if they wish to turn the clock backwards.

It can be noted that in the week after getting the games in July 2001, the Chinese arrested Chinese-American scholars on some rather nebulous spy charges. They were released, but it seems China has a slow learning curve. We should be ready to protest, we should seek to have the games become international games, but we should not boycott.

HNN, November 19, 2001

11. A Conservative Supports Reparations

The notion of paying reparations to selected groups of citizens as compensation for past social injustices is a very divisive issue. Advocates of reparations point to massive past wrongs that have lingering negative consequences for peoples. On the other hand, opponents of reparations suggest that the effects of the past misdeeds of generations ago are too diffuse to really be considered causal factors that deserve correction by today's generation. Also many in the aggrieved group do not display signs of the past abuses of their peoples. Also opponents point out that they (of the current generation) were not responsible for the past wrongs, as they were not even alive at the time of the wrongs, and in many cases their ancestors were not party to any of the wrongs either—indeed their ancestors may have themselves sacrificed to end the wrongs. The issue is divisive, yet perhaps a common ground can be found. Perhaps many who have opposed reparations for African Americans can find a rationale for their support. I have.

Reparations have been granted to some groups but only after long campaigns that were vigorously resisted. It took Japanese American citizens who were imprisoned in detention camps during World War Two simply because of their heritage several decades before settlements of $20,000 were given; and they were given only to the actual persons who were placed into America's "Concentration Camps."

Native Americans constantly fight for lands and the rights to use lands that were illegally taken away from their peoples generations ago. They have had some success, but it has been quite limited and heavily opposed. A 1946 land claims act allowed them to make cases for reparations, however, the act provided that a restoration of land ownership could not be a settlement option. Some Native Nations such as the Lakota Sioux are still struggling for a return of the Black Hills of South Dakota. They receive little sympathy from Non-Native policy makers.

William N. Thompson

Today many African Americans leaders advance claims for reparations because other Americans engaged in and supported (actively or passively) the ownership of slaves of African heritage over a period of 246 years, 1619-1865. However, I have not found the argument to be totally persuasive. One line of my heritage was not even present in the country during these years, another line did not—to my knowledge (and I certainly hope they did not)—participate in slave ownership, and that line did contribute soldiers who died fighting in the anti-slavery cause during the Civil War.

I cannot deny that my heritage included supporters—at least passive supporters—of slavery. But then my line includes people who probably did many wrongs. But they also include many peoples who were wronged. So it is with others too. To make the argument in the extreme, consider whether a Jewish concentration camp survivor now residing in the United States should shoulder financial responsibilities for the institution of slavery that ended seventy five years prior to the Holocaust. I accept these arguments, still I do support reparations on behalf of African Americans living today.

My support for reparations is not directed to the institution of slavery. Rather it is directed to a policy that is perpetuated TODAY, a policy that has come to be considered the "best" social program of the Twentieth Century, and still the most wonderful social policy on the books. The policy is the one that is loved by all liberal elements. It is the cornerstone of many Democratic Party platforms, political appeals, and political victories. Get ready liberals—the reason I support reparations for African Americans is because SOCIAL SECURITY IS A RACIST PROGRAM.

Social security has purposely drawn money out of African American communities and transferred it to white Americans. The money taken away from African Americans is money that could have gone to build vibrant capitalism in business ventures (allowing most African Americans to have a sense of identify with Republican economic policies), it could have been given to education programs

Parables from (a not quite) Paradise, NV 89154

for African Americans (even "the children"), and it could have gone for support of health programs for African Americans.

The argument I make is simple. The details are not in my hand, and therefore I make an admission (perhaps even fatal to my argument) that my point of view can change if the facts in their totality are different than I now believe. I invite others more knowledgeable about the details to either confirm my view or convince me of my errors—I can admit error, I am not running for office.

Also, and let me make this very clear, I am speaking ONLY to the retirement benefit portion of social security (of course, this is by far the biggest part of the social security program.)

I call social security "racist" because social security is a defined benefit pension program. This is in contrast with defined contribution programs. In defined benefit programs, participants (and/or their employers) give money into the program as they work. Workers take money out only as retirement benefits according to some formula—years of service, average wages, etc. But it is critical to know that they only take out benefits in retirement, and only while they enjoy that retirement (meaning they are ALIVE). If the person dies before retirement, ALL the money is forfeited as there is NO benefit. If the retiree dies only a short time after retirement begins, there are no other retirement benefits, any potential retirement funds are LOST—regardless of how much money the person has put into the program. Collateral benefits are available for surviving spouses—but that is a side issue not directly material to this argument.

Under a defined contribution program (such as the popular individual retirement account programs), the money from the individual worker (and/or employer) is placed into an account for the individual. It is put into an individual LOCK BOX with the worker's name on it. It is the worker's money—individually and ALWAYS. The money is invested. It cannot be taken out until retirement, and then it supports the retirement. However, if the worker dies before retirement, all moneys in the account go to the worker's estate.

Assuming there are no confiscatory death taxes, the full value of the moneys remain with the worker's family and in the worker's community. Under provisions of defined contribution plans, a worker could draw funds gradually from his/her LOCK BOX during retirement, so that if the worker dies soon—or whenever the worker dies—all remaining funds in the individual LOCK BOX go to the worker's family.

The social security program has no individual LOCK BOXES. It is simply a "rob Peter to pay Paul" program, or as some might call it a "Ponzi" scheme. Those who die give, those who live collect.

I call it "racist" for the simple reason that the program takes more from people who don't live as long, and gives money to people who live longer. African Americans have since the inception of the program in 1935 had decidedly shorter life spans than white people. This has to be very easy to understand. My cursory review of the Statistical Abstract tells me that the white life expectancy since 1935, at five year intervals ranged from four to eleven years longer than the life expectancy of African Americans.

If (an assumption) there have been ten million African Americans will full careers under Social Security since 1935, and they averaged lives six years shorter than whites, and average benefits for African Americans under Social Security were $4000 a year (admittedly it is difficult to find an average figure for a 60 year span)—then the collective African American community (vis-a-vis whites) has been shorted $240 billion dollars (6x4000x10,000,000). Reparations in this amount are required to right the wrong of this racially biased program which has been conducted during OUR lifetimes, and continues to be in operation today.

My plan of reparations also recognizes that other "poor" peoples also have shorter life spans and the plan should incorporate a regress of wrongs for these people collectively.

Step one must be to end the current program. social security must be restructured from a defined benefit to defined contribution plan. Under the defined contribution plan, a portion of funds would be given to the non-retirement aspects of social security (insurance for child benefits, etc.—note also, the argument here is not at all directed to Medicare, but could be). While I would support the notion of giving the individual worker has some control over investment instruments, as long as they are approved by investment agencies (S.E.C.), a sizeable portion of the funds should be put into very secure government securities. All the funds, however, will be LOCKED in the LOCK BOX for the individual.

Step two involves appropriations of a present day value of $240 billion dollars over the next 25 years for special programs designed to "right the wrong." I suggest that a new $50 billion a year be devoted to the following programs.

1. Programs to increase the life span of African Americans (and "poor" people generally). These would include medical research into diseases that disproportionally affect African Americans: blood pressure and heart disease research, strokes, diabetes, cycle cell anemia research.

2. Programs to purchase health insurance for uncovered African American children and children of all poor persons.

3. Preventive medicine health programs directed toward disadvantaged groups.

4. Food programs for poor schools that involve a mandate that unhealthy food be removed from such schools. (Get the junk food that murders children—albeit in their younger adult years—OUT).

5. Enhanced crime control programs for communities where life expectancies are compromised by violence and drug use.

6. Health services that will get people out of drug dependencies (also tobacco dependencies) are also in order.

7. Programs to enhance capitalist economic activity in poor communities which have been economically victimized by discriminatory Social Security extractions of their wealth.

8. Special grants and loans for businesses, and for skill training for locally owned businesses in the communities.

9. Special educational grants given to traditionally African American Colleges and Universities for scholarships and educational development programs designed to foster entrepreneurship. Other scholarships for African Americans who wish to direct their careers toward economic development of African American and/or poor communities.

10. Scholarships for medical training for doctors/health givers who will devote careers to these communities.

The funding would be made whether or not we had a budget surplus. The program of reparations would not give individual grants unrelated to the goals of health, education, and economic development. In no way would an individual entitlement be created by any of these programs. While many of the items suggested have been part of political agendas of both liberals and conservatives, I suggest that these programs be given an EXTRA $50 billion a year for their support. (Procedures would have to be taken to assure that the extra funding would REALLY be made—ergo, no political gimmicks).

I would also suggest that all these programs (the $50 billion extra funding) be absolutely Sunset-ed after 25 years, as by then the new defined contribution social security program would have removed the "racist" damages afflicted by the "greatest social program" in American history.

The collective African American community has been grievously wronged by social security. As government policy makers are very wise to actuarial facts, and have been since the onset of this program, there can be little doubt but that the wrongs have been intentional—they have certainly been afflicted with the full knowledge of social security policy makers. The wrongs must be righted. Reparations for African Americans are in order.

TP, October 23, 2000; and HNN, September 5, 2001

William N. Thompson

12. Reparations, Retribution, or Just Plain Bad Karma: The Fugimori Interlude in Peru Continues

The rather strange, or we should say "bizarre," regime of Alberto Fugimori as president and past-president of Peru continues, while the leader known as "El Chino" lives in exile in Japan. The events of the Fugimori Interlude did not just fall out of the sky onto Peru as if a meteorite coming from outer space. The events have real life origins overlooked yet deserving of some examination and evaluation.

Alberto Fugimori was born in Peru (purportedly) in 1938. His parents were Japanese immigrants. Population pressures and economic problems (especially the effects of the Depression) in Japan led to a major exodus from the Islands. Japanese went in many directions with large numbers coming to the Americas, most to the United States, but among other nations Peru was a leading host country. (Gardiner; Klaren).

Peru needed laborers, especially for farm work, and also for factory production in Amazon rubber region. Many came with contracts forcing them to work for several years. However, when contracts ended, the immigrants gravitated toward urban life in Lima and the industrial port suburb of Callao. As these immigrants gained personal independence they turned to work in which they could utilize specialized skills they had developed in Japan. They created small businesses and they very willingly competed with existing Peruvian entrepreneurs. Their savvy business skills incurred the wrath of many in their host nation.

Emigration from Japan increased in the early 1930s, and Peruvian officials responded to pressures from Peruvian business interests to stop a wave of new competition. In 1936 Peru's congress passed a new immigration law. The law drastically restricted the flow of Japanese entering the country. Racial "group" immigration was prohibited. Quotas were placed on immigrants returning to Japan and then re-entering Peru. Immigrants were allowed to comprise only 20% of any profession or trade skill area. After the law was passed, Japan officially protested. However, the Peruvian Foreign Minister refused to receive the protest, stating that the law applied to all other nations and not just Japan. However, Foreign Minister Ulloa proclaimed at the time that "their (the Japanese) conditions and methods of working have produced pernicious competition for Peruvian workers." The effect of the law was to stem Japanese migrations; however, there were loopholes in the law. Many immigrants hastened to become Peru citizens so they could be excluded from the quotas. (Connell, Gardiner; Klaren; Weglyn).

Hostilities persisted. There were many demonstrations against the Japanese. Then, on May 13, 1940, things turned ugly. A protest became a full scale riot. Shops were attacked, looted and burned. Rioters also assaulted Japanese residents. Over 600 structures were damaged, with property losses approaching two million dollars. Ten Japanese were killed, while scores were injured. Japan held Peru responsible. However, the government declined to accept blame, with officials even suggesting that the Japanese provoked the riots. Less than a week later the government issued a decree which temporarily suspended all immigration. That might have been bad, but the worst was yet to come. (Connell; Gardiner).

Soon nations of the Americas were swept into the events of World War Two. Right after the attack on Pearl Harbor. the U.S. Ambassador to Peru told the foreign minister that the situation with Peru would be "delicate" as the country had "so prominent" a Japanese colony. In January 1942, Peru cut off relations with Japan and other Axis nations. (They declared war on Germany and Japan in 1945.) But the United States wanted more. The United States was allowed to establish an airfield at Talara, Peru. Our nation soon developed what in retrospect can be called a paranoia regarding Japanese immigrants (and descendants of immigrants) to the Americas. (Klaren).

The American hunt for "dangerous" Japanese went beyond our own borders. It involved the cooperation of many of the governments of the Americas. Other governments included the Peruvians, Bolivia, Chile, Costa Rica, Dominican Republic, Colombia, El Salvador, Haiti, Honduras, Mexico, Nicaragua, Panama and Venezuela. These nations were asked to round-up key Japanese leaders and exile them to the United States for confinement. Most did so half-heartedly at best. Peru responded with enthusiasm. Eighty per cent of those expelled to be imprisoned in the United States were from Peru. Estimated suggest that as many as 2280 Peruvians were shipped to the United States. (Connell; Gardiner).

Among other motivations, the United States government, according to Michi Weglyn's Years of Infamy (1976) wanted additional persons of Japanese-origins in its detention camps in order to use them in offers for prisoner exchanges or exchanges for American civilians in Japan or elsewhere. It did not matter that the Japanese were Peruvians and in some cases Peru citizens—at least they were not U. S. citizens. Actually there may have been a desire that they not be Peruvian "citizens." The U.S. State Department suggested to President Manual Prado of Peru that a law for denaturalization of naturalized Peru citizens could facilitate their expulsion and transportation to the United States.

The United States paid all expenses in the round-ups and transportation to the detainment camps. The first ship left the Port of Lima (Callao) on April 5, 1942 carrying 141 Japanese Peruvians. Actually 80 went "voluntarily," that is, they claimed a desire to leave, fearing further violence against their persons and property in Peru. (Connell).

Actually protection of their property was a "moot point," as the government of President Prado had seized most Japanese-Peruvian property including a large cotton ranch and a saw mill. The president distributed much of the property to personal friends. A second ship took 342 out in June. These early ships also carried Germans and Italians under somewhat similar circumstances.

These voluntarily and "kidnapped" passengers were moved first to Kennedy, Texas where they were placed in an abandoned CCC camp. Later some were moved to Seagoville, Texas, or Santa Fe, New Mexico. But the largest number including those in later shiploads went to Crystal City, Texas, 110 miles south of San Antonio. There they were placed into what was previously a migrant work camp. The camp also held 1000 Germans.

Eight hundred of the Japanese "not quite" prisoners of war from Peru were actually exchanged for American prisoners of war held by the Japanese nation. Others were encouraged to return to Japan "voluntarily." Many reluctantly did so when arrangements were made to have members of their families still residing in Peru also sent to Japan. (Connell).

After the end of the War, Peru refused (until 1953) to accept a return of any of these Peruvian-Japanese internees who had been held in the United States, or who had been sent to Japan. They encouraged that the ones still in the United States be sent to the now war-devastated Japan although most had never set foot on Japanese soil in their lifetimes. Others remained confined in the American internment camps well into 1946. The United States government finally acquiesced to allow hundreds to remain in the United States as "freed" persons who eventually could become citizens. A large contingent, over 200 in number, went to Seabrook Farms in New Jersey. They were given $25 and a railroad ticket from Texas. There they were farm workers along with many new refugees from Europe. (Connell; Gardiner).

All these internees from Peru (whether Japanese, German, or Italian) were non-(U.S.A.) Americans. Therefore, they have not been prominent on the radar screen when the injustices to internees is engaged as an issue. Crystal City is not even considered one of our ten U. S. internee camps. Also the oversight supports the continuing myth that we did not hold Germans or Italians in internment. We did. They were civilians, but they were not U.S. citizens. They were Peruvians.

William N. Thompson

After decades of pressure from Japanese Americans for some justice, along with support from myriad civil rights contingents, congress passed a Reparations Act in 1988. It was signed by President Reagan on August 10, 1988. Each surviving detainee from a Japanese-American internment camp was given $20,000. (Hatamiya; Connell).

However, in 1993, Attorney General Janet Reno decreed that no grant would be given to the Peruvian internees, even to those who remained in the United States. She read the Act to apply only to citizens of the United States or to resident aliens. She determined that when the Peruvian-Japanese were brought to the United States, they were not citizens but rather "illegal aliens," albeit they were brought here by American vessels at a cost to the American government, and with a modicum of force. (Vazquez).

In 1997 members of congress asked President Clinton to include the Latin American internees in the reparation payments, but he declined, saying he was not empowered to define the group into the provisions of the 1988 Act. (Connell). However, as the result of a court action, in 1998, the department of justice agreed that the Peruvian detainees could receive $5000 each.

Six hundred pressed claims, but 1300 were eligible for the one-fourth shares. Sort of reverts one's mind back to the days of the constitutional convention, where one group of Americans was considered a fraction of the worth—in that case 3/5th—of another American. There is a continued campaign seeking full equity in reparations for these Americans (and other Peruvians internees). (Vasquez; CNN.com, June 12, 1998).

The equity answer may now reside in Japan. After an 11 year reign of Alberto Fugimori, the Peruvian president abandoned his land in November 2000 for a self-imposed exile in Japan. As he left, charges were renewed—now officially—that he had engaged in a long campaign of corruption and theft of monies from the public treasury and other funds, including charity money given to Peru for social causes by residents of Japan. (<u>New York Times</u>, November 26,

2000). His "thefts" were considered to be as much as ten million dollars or more. His chief advisor profited so much from thefts and drug money that his frozen bank accounts had $70 million in deposits. A Fugimori military leader had a Swiss account of $14.5 million, while $9 billion from the sale of government businesses to further Fugimori policies of privatization also seemed to have disappeared. (New York Times, November 23, 2000; April 29, 2001; January 30, 2001; June 20, 2002).

Fugimori sought and won Japanese citizenry, claiming that his parents registered him as a Japanese citizen when he was born in 1938. Some Peruvians support the rumor that he may have actually been born in Japan—but as Peru did not allow Japanese immigration after 1936 (until the 1950s), that is unlikely. (New York Times, January 11, 2002). Nonetheless, in a country where it is a difficult and long path for a non-native son to win citizenship, Fugimori was made a citizen within a month of his arrival in exile.

Japan refuses to extradite their new citizen as a matter of general policy. They say if he is a criminal, he will be subject to their justice system. (New York Times, June 28, 2001). Ironically, Fugimori has, some say, expressed a desire to return to Peru and seek the presidency again. He has also explored running for a seat in Japan's Diet. (New York Times, January 11, 2002).

Perhaps he should be allowed to run for president again. Former president Alan Garcia, was charged with political corruption and theft after he departed to Colombia and France where he remained in exile during Fugimori's reign. But in 2001 he returned and he was allowed to run for president, as a prodigal son returned. Peru's supreme court had ruled that a statue of limitations had run its course. (New York Times, July 14, 2001).

However, should the court permit a return in a condition other than in handcuffs, Fugimori's should be required to make a full return of the money he stole. But the money should not go back to Peru. The money should go to his fellows of Japanese heritage who received only 25% of their due compensation, as well as others who were sent to Japan—-for the indignities as well as the property losses incurred at hands of Peru government—and the government of the United States. If he returns but $19.5 million, reparations for the 1300 "eligibles" could be fully funded. Indeed, one might speculate that Fugimori's indiscretions (the financial ones) were but an alternative method for directing reparations to Japanese Peruvians of the World War II era. Equity is still required.

(Source Material: Thomas Connell, American Japanese Hostages, 2002; C. Harvey Gardiner, The Japanese and Peru, 1975; Leslie Hatamiya, Righting a Wrong; Peter Klaren, Peru, 2000; Richard L. Vazquez, "Justice for Japanese Latinos," www.LasCulturas.com, 2000; Michi Weglyn, Years of Infamy, 1976.)

HNN, January 13, 2003

13. Hiroshima Reflections

I. My "Truths" About the Bomb

1. What did they expect: IT'S CALLED WAR! It ain't beanbag!

2. THEY started it.

3. They deserved PAYBACK for their "sneaky" little attack on Pearl Harbor.

4. You better believe it. THEY WOULD HAVE DONE IT TO US if they had had the chance.

5. What's their beef? MORE DIED in the fire bombings of DRESDEN and TOKYO. Why do they think Hiroshima and Nagasaki are so special?

6. The JAPANESE ATROCITIES in China, Korea, and Southeast Asia including rapes and pillage of civilian populations deserved some kind of retribution. We had to get the point across that this would NEVER be tolerated ever again.

7. How can the bomb be criticized considering WHAT THE JAPANESE DID TO THEIR WAR PRISONERS? They broke every civilized rule of war.

8. WE SAVED LIVES by dropping the bombs. Over one million American military would have lost their lives in an invasion of Japan. The loss of one single American life would have been unconscionable knowing we had the bomb that would end the war immediately. One single American life saved was worth all the Japanese lives lost with the two bombs.

9. How many Japanese lives did we SAVE by using the bombs? Probably millions—military and civilian. If we would have had to invade Japan, they would have engaged in a fight to the finish for their mainland.

10. We had to END THE WAR QUICKLY, because Japanese suicide pilots were attacking our Navy ships as they approached the Japanese mainland.

11. If the bomb was so bad, why didn't they surrender after Hiroshima? Why did THEY make us drop a second bomb?

12. It is a bit much to have THEM talk about the sanctity of life. KAMIKAZE isn't exactly an American word. It was THEY who had the suicide bombers. Our leaders didn't do Hara-kari when things went wrong.

13. This revisionism is quite insincere. Sometimes people just want to knock the United States. WE ARE THE GREATEST COUNTRY IN HISTORY, and Harry TRUMAN, without a doubt, was the greatest president during our lifetimes anyway. Thank God! We had a man with guts in office when we needed him!

II. Other Views

1. The atomic bomb involved secret (illegal) budgeting games by congress and the president. The investment in the project was very large ($2-3 billion), and if it had failed a lot of congressmen just might have gone to the slammer. We HAD TO JUSTIFY spending the money on the bomb project by proving the bomb could actually work in a wartime situation.

2. We had to show Russia just who was going to be in charge after the war. Already Russia had shown signs of opposition to its democratic war allies. If we had not demonstrated to Russia that we had the power of the bomb on our side, Russia might have tried to start a cold war with us. Such an engagement could have tied up our military and national financial resources for over half a century.

3. We made an agreement with Russia that they would come into the Asian theater of the War 90 days after the War ended in Europe. We thought we needed their help, because we did not know the bomb would be successful. Now we didn't need their help. But if they got into the Asian War before we could end it, they would try to

be included in the surrender negotiations, and they would want some of the spoils of the Asian War. Those spoils had been earned. They belonged to the U.S. of A., lock, stock, and barrel, not to any Commie-come-lately Russians. The Hiroshima bombing was August 6, 1945. As THEY AGREED TO DO, Russia declared war on Japan on August 8, 1945, exactly 90 days after the war ended in Europe.

4. Our military leaders had shown incompetence in the manner in which they allowed massive numbers of American lives to be wasted in defeats of the Japanese on islands such as Iwo Jima and Okinawa. We had lost sight of military objectives and demanded at each engagement that we defeat the enemy completely regardless of the objective sought. We used the massive number of American military casualties in the Pacific engagements to formulate our estimates of the numbers of personnel that would be lost in a Japanese mainland invasion. We did not calculate costs for winning any objective which did not include a complete capitulation on the part of both the Japanese military and its civilian homeguard.

5. We had to make the atomic bomb drops without any specific warnings, because Japan would have only hardened its resistance to the American military if we had said we would drop a bomb and then did not do so, or did so and the bomb failed to work.

6. If we would have announced targets for the bomb, the Japanese would have only moved prisoners of war to the sites.

7. We only had three bombs. We used one in New Mexico. We did not have anymore for demonstrations or testing. We had to use the bombs on Japanese targets to demonstrate to Japan that we would destroy the entire country if they did not capitulate.

8. We needed fresh unbombed targets in order to assess the damage the bomb could inflict on structures. After four targets were selected, they became off-limits for conventional bombing.

9. We needed the scientific knowledge that would come from analyzing the effects of using the bomb on people, hence we had to use it on a populated area.

III. More Thoughts

1. The bomb(s) was developed because we feared that Hitler would make one and we had to check his power. We did not have any concern that Japan would develop a nuclear weapon. Part of the research community included Jewish refugees who wished to have a weapon of retaliation against Hitler. The bomb was never intended for use against Japan. The scientific community did not accept that Japanese atrocities justified such retaliation as the bomb delivered. An element of the scientific community became very much opposed to nuclear weapons when the object of their planned use became the Soviet Union.

2. Our goal was to stop the war. We therefore had to drop the bomb in such a way that we could convince the warlords that they should accept surrender. However, we did not wish to drop the bomb on the warlords, because we wanted THEM to survive (1) so that they could order the surrender, and (2) so we could try them and kill them.

3. We chose targets that were far from the warlords' headquarters (Tokyo). Yet we wanted them to react to the bomb—to totally surrender in accordance with a policy we had developed at Potsdam several weeks earlier. We dropped the bomb on Hiroshima. The main communication links between Hiroshima and Tokyo were broken. The first reports that reached the warlords indicated a new bigger bomb had been dropped, but the reports minimized the damage. The reports were probably consistent with the rules of communication, i.e., that bad news has a difficult time travelling upstream in communication channels. More accurate reports of the devastation and the extent of structural and human damage reached the warlords on August 9, at precisely the same time we were dropping the second bomb on Nagasaki.

4. We did a great job at selection of target locations. The first bomb went off (hypocenter) directly above the Shima Hospital in Hiroshima. (Shima means island). The second bomb went off (hypocenter) directly above the Catholic Hospital of Nagasaki. Most of the medical response capacity of both cities was destroyed in the bombings. As doctors worked in the cities, there were few surviving physicians in either place who were available to care for the wounded and those ill from atomic disease.

5. The targets had no enduring military value, although both cities did house factories and military installations. The United States and its allies had complete command of the air. Frequent air raid alerts were sounded in the cities as American planes (B-29s) flew missions over the cities uncontested. The factories of the towns were completely at the mercy of the American bombers. Any wartime production capacity that remained in the cities had already been completely neutralized. The cities may have been targeted because their populations had engaged in wartime production which at a previous time was adverse to our military threat. In such case our bombings may have been retaliatory.

6. Nagasaki was the one open city of Japan during the three century Togagawa regime—1600s-1800s. Nagasaki had a Dutch trade center, and the city allowed Christian missionaries. The Christian presence remained after the Meigi regime emerged in the mid-Nineteenth Century. Not only was Nagasaki the center of Christian activity in Japan, it was also a place where anti-war sentiment was most loudly expressed.

7. The Japanese did make overtures to the Russians months earlier. Certain leaders expressed a desire for Russian assistance in opening up communication channels with the United States so that discussions to end the war could be undertaken. Russia was not overtly helpful because they knew that they would soon enter the war and they wanted to be able to pick up some of the spoils.

8. After Potsdam, the United States offered an imprecise ultimatum asking for total surrender and indicating that the United States would destroy Japan if the Japanese leaders did not surrender. The ultimatum made no precise mention of a super bomb or that such would be used on Japanese cities.

9. The date for an invasion of Japan was set. The invasion would begin on November 1, 1945. The bombs were dropped on August 6 and August 9.

10. The property loss suffered by the residents of Hiroshima and Nagasaki was the combined equivalent of the annual wages of 1.2 million Japanese workers. The people who lost property had to "fend for themselves." They did not have government grants or loans. There was no program to help with property losses. The United States through General MacArthur (American Caesar) was THE government of Japan after the war, THE government that gave no help.

11. The number of casualties in terms of deaths and injuries in the two bombings approached one half a million or more. For the wounded and sick survivors there was no medical aid program at all. They had to "fend for themselves" until the Atomic Bomb Medical Treatment Law was passed in 1957. The Japanese government was very remiss in not attending to the special needs of these people (no other Japanese suffered from atomic bomb disease—with Leukemia, keloids, cancer from bombings). But then it was the United States that served as THE government of Japan in the immediate years after the war.

12. The United States as THE government of Japan did have post war policies regarding the dropping of the two bombs. The United States government censured all mention of the bombs in the Japanese Press, we forbade all discussion of the bomb in Japanese schools (after all, WE had to re-educate the Japanese so that THEY could become democratic), we allowed no public display of photographs or of art work depicting Hiroshima or Nagasaki or their

residents after the bombings. Maybe, the fact that the restored government of Japan lagged in its duties to help these people (point 10 and 11 above) could be partially—at least a little—excused because the entire population of Japan just wasn't told.

13. IF the bomb was necessary, IF the bomb was the way to a quick end of the War, IF the bomb saved millions of lives—American AND JAPANESE, IF the bomb was so GOOD, WHY WAS THE POLICY OF OUR GOVERNMENT DIRECTED TOWARD CENSORING DISCUSSION AND DISPLAYS ABOUT THE BOMBINGS OF HIROSHIMA AND NAGASAKI?

HNN, August 14, 2001

William N. Thompson

14. Being Number One Means Never Having to Say You're Sorry: A Picture from Panama

We're Number One! We're Number One! We're Number One! And don't ever let anyone think differently; or at least don't let on that reality could be any different.

New Year's Day is not just for football games and the championship bowl alliance, it is also a day to make resolutions, and this New Year's Day, it is a day to keep them. The United States is recognizing the sovereignty of the Panamanian peoples over lands quickly acquired (through a questionable treaty) by the United States after supporting a military revolution in Panama in 1903. While we renegotiated an understanding in a 1977 treaty which returns the canal zone lands within Panama to the people of that country, we are not giving the lands back with any sense of magnanimity or in recognition that justice may now be served by publicly recognizing the concept of political self-determination—something we have espoused at other times in our history. The president of the United States could not have his schedule interrupted by the notion of having to make a day's excursion to Panama to help honor the peoples who acquiesced in our control and operations of the canal for over 85 years in their territory. A vice president had campaign commitments. A secretary of state just had to be somewhere else. A presidential wife was building her fence around her New York mansion. Quite simply there was nothing in it for us (for our leaders) to participate in another country's achievement of full sovereignty.

On the other hand, there are some voices still heard in the land suggesting that we never should have agreed to let the Panamanians have a restoration of their sovereignty. Opposition to the 1977 treaty does persist, and there can be little doubt that a focus group of citizens might have suggested this is not a matter that our consensus political leaders should be highlighting by their activities.

There have been good feelings in Panama about the United States over the past few years. We have cooperated with the economic leaders in the land to help them establish and reinforce a basis upon which they can continue to strive for prosperity. Many of the sad episodes of the past—episodes not entirely erased—including several unilateral military incursions onto the lands of Panama and other Central American countries as well as Mexico have drifted to the back of the collective memories of the people. Economic domination of the country's resources by the United States and other outside countries no longer provokes "Yankee Go Home" sentiments in any overt manner. Indeed the people have become super New York "Yankees" fans as their own talented players are recognized by us as our "most valuable."

So why can't we bow and show grace as we honor a commitment to "give something up," albeit something that never was "ours"—another people's sovereignty? Our lack of grace is a slap in the face of history. But more than that, it is lost opportunity to lay a foundation for a new alliance for cooperation with Latin America. It is too bad that our president could not see a political constituency within the United States that he could pander to with a show of concession. After all, he has apologized for slavery—a condition for which no living American bears a personal responsibility. He apologized for troubles in Rwanda and Burundi, although no living American bears a personal responsibility for the internecine genocide in those lands. He pardoned Puerto Rican terrorists, as if it were wrong to keep such people in captivity. Of course, in all these cases there were constituencies that could be massaged to the benefit of the president, his political vice president and political wife.

Of course, our leaders can cry out in protest that Middle East peace talks must take precedence over ceremonies in Panama, but then again, we seem to have constituencies and voters that propel that priority (and really, how many peace talks have there been anyway, like won't next week have another round). Panama demanded one day. It might also be suggested that the paternalistic notion that only daddy U.S.A. is capable of convincing peoples not to war with each other is becoming a little old.

Maybe our leaders' are having flashbacks. Could Panama be viewed as another Vietnam? Could our honoring of a commitment and treaty be seen as some sort of shame that we must not expose to the light of day. We know that individually our leaders in recent years have no capacity for shame, but must their personal postures become our national tradition—or perhaps, are their personal postures just a reflection of what has become our national tradition. Presidential historians have recently showed their reverence for Teddy Roosevelt and his unrelentless gingoism. Maybe we should revere some other images.

Our Panama reaction can be contrasted with that shown by Great Britain just two years ago when with all the pomp and circumstances of royalty that could be summoned from the depths by a fading monarchy, old flags were lowered and new flags raised in Hong Kong. We know the Chinese leaders are not very nice people, but at least the British had the courtesy to bow. Our Panama reaction is more akin to our stonewall of denial and silence over the motivations for bombing the Chinese embassy during our recent war in Belgrade.

Other nations know shame, and know when to back off of arrogance. Certainly our World War Two adversaries tried to hide and deny their atrocities. They certainly don't wave the flag in celebration of their inhumanities. In contrast we try to justify our wrongs (or more delicately our "questionable" activities) not in terms of human mistakes and frailties, but rather by redefinitions and national righteousness. An atomic bomb that wastes hundreds of thousands of lives is redefined as a tool "that saved a million lives." Instead of examining its use in the context of an emotional policy frenzy fraught with a lack of good information, we turn it into a flag waving event. A pilot in the actual bombing recreates the event for a bicentennial audience.

At the Smithsonian Museum, questions about the wisdom of the decision to use the bomb are censored from the display of the plane that first delivered its terror upon civilians. The Nevada state legislature passes a resolution requesting the return of the plane to its hangar location in the town of Wendover, because the Enola Gay can be a featured attraction to draw even more tourists to Nevada—the entertainment capital of the world. Joe Lewis told us that we could not lose the war, because "God is on our side." And if God is on our side, how can we possibly do anything wrong, or even questionable.

In another piece I commented upon the career of President Harding, a man who is never lifted up by our historians as a model for our little school children. However, my comments recognized that when he viewed wrongs being done by those about him, he became a broken man—broken in spirit, and truly broken in health. He demonstrated true signs of remorse. Why can't we as a nation learn the things the Robert Fulgrum learned in kindergarten—"don't hit people, and put back things where you found them?" We have come a long way, or perhaps we have not come very far at all. Our president didn't skip a beat as he was personally disgraced by his own conduct. Instead he organized his political resources in a concerted attack upon those who might question his conduct, an attack now being played out in a prosecution of a person who gathered evidence about his wrong doing. Meanwhile he goes on his world legacy tour of 1999-2000, building peace (we can hope) among those in the Middle East, and apologizing whenever the pollsters and focus groups say it is good for his ratings and those of his candidate sidekicks, and dancing so nimbly and quick around any display that might be interpreted as not being in his immediate political interest. "We're Number One, Don't Ever Forget it." I guess that is the legacy that we all may be leaving the world as our term as the world's unquestioned and unquestionable best nation continues unabated into the next millennium. We leave the millennium without any demonstration that we as a people have learned anything from the story of humility, the story of the man who defined time on our calendars at the beginning of the last millennium.

TP, December 20, 1999.

William N. Thompson

15. Warren Harding—Maybe it's Time for a Eulogy

I was in the Blackbird Pub in Croughton Village, England, where I was resident while teaching with the U.S. Air Force. One of the many regulars approached me in a friendly way and asked what I thought about this Reagan thing. "What do you mean?" I replied. The crusty old gentleman answered, "Why, it's on the news, your president fell asleep while having an audience with the Pope." "Oh," I responded, "He's done that in cabinet meetings too." "Well, our Maggie would never do that," he offered. He asked me what I thought of Maggie Thatcher, and I indicated that I thought she was very bright and quick on her feet, that she could carry any debate on any topic without having a speech scripted out like our president did. I added that she would never fall asleep on the job. "Well," he said, "What does that tell you about our two countries then?" I answered, "Quite simply, it tells me that you need leaders, and we don't."

But alas, our nation has once more been saturated by an onslaught of media hero-worship as the John F. Kennedy Jr. tragedy has played itself out. We have been told again of Camelot, and we have been told that here was our new "prince," the one we had been waiting for, one who surely would be able to quickly make a move to be a U.S. senator and then after a term, or part of a term, would be ready to be our president. I am glad that I don't have to go into the Blackbird Pub tonight, for it I repeated my words, they might sound quite anti-American—at the moment anyway. Fortunately we do not have to live "at the moment" for too long. The Kennedy worship shall not last much beyond the appropriate time for showing proper respect, that is, until the next celebrity event comes along be it a murder trial, seventy-five home runs, or a political sex scandal. We are also fortunate that the C-Span television network has given us new perspectives and insights on the lives and times of all the presidents in a fantastic series that is being shown throughout the year. We have not been told by the those producing this series that we must worship the historians' favorites—Washington, Jefferson, Lincoln, Wilson, the Roosevelts, and Truman. Nor are we told that we must relegate the other presidents to an almost Soviet-esque status as non-persons in History. Rather we are permitted to observe all the presidencies and discover "new" things which were hidden before by the hero-worshipers of academic departments of history. We learn, for instance, of the personal trials of a Franklin Pierce who missed the golden ring because his primary goal in office was to avoid a bloody war the consequences of which still divide the nation. We learned that the "historically-maligned" Ulysses S. Grant was truly a reforming spirit and in no ways a corrupt bungler.

I sincerely hope that this series can bring a sense of redefinition of performance standards in the presidency. Perhaps then we can begin to accept the notion that steady diligence and honest efforts in the job certainly count as much as sloganeering and political posturing for historical portrait-makers. (The ultimate example of such pandering to historians was made by a president who actually hired an historian to be on his staff—not just any historian, but an historian who was the son of the very historian who created "polls" to determine presidential greatness). Perhaps then we can reach even so deep into the barrel of the "unworthy" as the presidency of Warren G. Harding and find reason for a tribute to replace the almost universal derision found in our popular social studies school books.

We have just marked the 76th anniversary of the death (August 2, 1999) of our country's 28th President, Warren Gamaliel Harding. For over three-quarters of a century the history writing establishment has repeatedly vilified this man for his shortcomings, factual and fictional. The very real accomplishments of his administration have been almost totally overlooked or belittled, while the "legitimate" gatekeepers to the ranks of "presidential greatness," whatever that is, have permanently barred the doors to Harding as they almost unanimously confine him to the ranks of the "failed." Perhaps his fate at the hands of our intellectual guardians was to be expected. After all, he had to follow one of the "greats" or "near greats," Thomas Woodrow Wilson, and he served just a few years before the "undisputed great" Franklin Delano Roosevelt. He is also faulted for having won the 1920 election against Democrat James Cox and his running mate, Franklin Delano Roosevelt.

William N. Thompson

Maybe after 76 years, Warren Gamaliel Harding deserves a tribute, not a trashing. This essay cannot be a complete account, but it can offer a selection of accomplishments that should be viewed beside the often reported personal weaknesses (guess what—of the flesh), and the misdeeds and violations of the public trust of certain of his appointees (but never misdeeds that in any way suggested that he was a personal financial benefactor of that mistrust).

Not only do the accomplishments represent major milestones in the history of the presidency, but ironically they portray a man who, while labeled a staunch conservative advocate of a "normalcy" somewhat akin to an attachment to Genghis Khanism or Attila the Hunism, may have been much the "liberal" that the historians should admire.

Case in point number one. Harding did not follow a great social liberal in office. He followed a racist. This he was not. While Harding vacillated on issues of race (like Kennedy did not?) he did give strong support to an anti-lynching bill, and he did something else. On October 26, 1921, he travelled to Birmingham, Alabama, and gave a speech publicly endorsing the end of economic, political, or educational discrimination. It was the first time since the Civil War that a president had spoken out so vigorously on behalf of positive race relations.

Harding was a man who promoted peace. Wilson provided "ideals" but was very short on results. The Wilsonian "ideals" gave us a new nation, Yugoslavia. Harding had results—that is, more meaningful results. While the historians like to give the credit for his positive accomplishments to his Secretary of State Charles Evans Hughes, he chose Hughes, and the accomplishments were on his watch. Moreover it was not Hughes that pardoned "war protestor" Eugene V. Debs, it was Harding. Wilson had jailed Debs in a vindictive and war hysteria move against the famous labor leader. Harding's administration also called the Washington Naval Conference which was the first international disarmament conference during peacetime in the history of the world. The last time I noticed, disarmament was still on the national political agenda.

Harding had been a small town businessman and he showed definite policy preferences for business-favorable government. He lowered taxes and he cut the federal budget, in a sense offering a policy motif followed by great supply-siders the likes of John F. Kennedy and Ronald Reagan. Nonetheless, Harding was not unsympathetic with the workers of America. His secretary of commerce called a national conference on unemployment (the first of its kind) in 1921. Perhaps the conference was the precursor of the Humphrey-Hawkins reports much heralded by latter-day liberals. And in 1922 Harding intervened in a steel strike with support that led to the acceptance of the eight hour day. His arguments on behalf of a U.S. department of public welfare were certainly ahead of their time, as was his advocacy of federal regulation of aviation and the radio air waves, issues that quite obviously still need some resolution.

Harding did feel that government should be run like a business. He oversaw the passage of the Budget Reform Act of 1921 which created not only a bureau of the budget but also the general accounting office. Wilson had on the one hand verbalized support for such a rationalization of financial policy making, but on the other hand had vetoed the legislation creating the agency which prepares the federal budget. The power-monger Wilson could not fathom that the auditing function of budgeting be in non-executive hands, ergo with a G.A.O. reporting to Congress. Only after Charles Dawes was appointed to be budget director in 1921, did the United States have an annual consolidated federal budget document.

In the interest of good management practices, congress also passed the historic Job Classification Act of 1923—during his administration. The goal of the act was "equal pay for equal work," certainly a rally cry we have heard in recent months.

To be sure there were policies that would make today's liberals cringe—he did not allow a soldiers bonus, he failed to recognize the government of the Soviet Union, he acquiesced in the passage of an immigration quota act, and he was for high tariffs. He also committed the sins of being conciliatory, pleasant, compromising, and indeed passive on many issues. After the two administrations of the very domineering Wilson, Harding purposely chose another leadership style. He respected congress. Moreover, he inwardly realized that his job was much bigger than he was. The true danger of having hero-leaders is they cannot see any limits to their power being in the public interest.

Harding could see that he was limited in talent, something that the "strong" "the great" presidents seldom see when they contemplate themselves. Therefore he relied upon others—mortal giants like Charles Evans Hughes, Herbert Hoover, and William Howard Taft, the former president whom he named as chief justice of the Supreme Court. He surrounded himself with others who were competent as well—Dawes and Secretary of the Treasury Andrew Mellon.

But alas he also surrounded himself with political hacks who turned out to be quite dishonest persons, persons who chose to steal from the resources of the public for their personal enrichment.

As his administration progressed into its second and third years, the deeds of his dishonest "friends" began to emerge.

And here the true mark of the man Harding could be seen as well. The emerging scandals provided a very heavy burden and stress upon the man. For his entire administration he had labored under a weak physical condition with constantly high blood pressure. No historian has ever demonstrated that Harding knew of the scandals in which his friends were involved; no record suggests that he ever benefitted from the thievery of his friends. Quite to the contrary, the strain of scandal disturbed him deeply, and observers could tell that the strain was breaking his health. Although there was a measure of mystery surrounding his death, he had experienced a decided decline in health prior to his demise. That decline was an outward manifestation that this man knew shame. And that perhaps is a quality of greatness our nation has not witnessed its chief executives for some time. A little genuine display of shame could have left our incumbent president in a more honorable light with his non-historian contemporaries—if they count in the equation.

Warren Gamaliel Harding, 28th President of the United States of America. A person who made many positive contributions as a leader, a person who allowed others to make many positive contributions under his leadership. A person betrayed by trusted friends, a person broken and shamed by his own inadequacies in controlling others, in assessing the qualities of others.

Warren Gamaliel Harding does not deserve to be a saint, and he should not be worshipped as a hero, but he was a president who is part of the nation's history. His administration was not a Camelot; he did not seek celebrity status; he did not relish notoriety; he did not have to impress upon the nation that he was the "leader." He was not a bad person, he did not do bad public things. He deserves better than he has been given by the historians of our land. In the spirit of truth-seeking evidenced in the series of features on all the presidents, he at least merits a measure of historical respect.

TP, September 15, 1999

William N. Thompson

16. Rating Presidential Greatness—Ratings Bunk

Suffering through the Y2K litany of "The Greatest" this and that of the millennium and the century, I was not impressed with the discussion of American leaders. Show after show featured historians expounding the same drivel we have been fed ever since we opened our high school history books. Franklin Delano Roosevelt "saved the free enterprise system" (although panels admitted our economic distress was as great in 1939 as it was in 1933 when he took office). Franklin Delano Roosevelt "humanized" government (with programs such as public housing). Franklin Delano Roosevelt saved Democracy both here and in the world (although the panels admitted he gave eastern Europe to Stalin).

Albert Einstein was seen as the greatest man of the century because he helped give us the "bomb," the accomplishment that was "the greatest." And of course Harry Truman remained a "great one," with his forceful decision making, such as using the "bomb," albeit there was no mention of the civilians who were on the ground to receive the greatest gift. And, of course, we heard again of Woodrow Wilson, who gave us the League of Nations (no mention that the Iroquois Nations came up with the same idea four centuries ago).

Lincoln, Jefferson, Washington—nothing new, no serious questioning, no insights beyond half-truths and false myths we have had shoved down our throats as part of our public school "civic" education since early childhood. Clearly, the millennium assessments presented to us by our major media sources qualified to be labeled ones of "Presidential Cults and Cultists."—the title of the first chapter of Thomas Bailey's 1966 book, <u>Presidential Greatness</u>. In the book, Bailey reviews the attempts of historians to make lists of our presidents from best to worse, from the greatest to near great, to average, to failures.

Bailey reveals the "cults" surrounding the darlings of biased panelists, noting that liberals, Democrats, and the Harvard educated are disproportionately represented. Ergo: in 1945 a general public poll of "greatest" Americans overlooks Andrew Jackson, but in the same year Arthur Schlesinger Jr. writes a glowing history of Jackson and wins the Pulitzer Prize. Arthur Schlesinger, Sr., conducts a poll of historians in 1948 and Jackson is now listed as a "Great." The Jackson cult emerges.

Bailey makes a strong case against the listings, offering insights overlooked by myth-makers, and exposing their obvious biases—thrashing Republicans for personal moral shortcomings, and completely overlooking the same character deficiencies in their "favorites"; deploring conditions of the downtrodden, but applauding those leading us in wars to expand slavery; loving civil liberties, but praising those who have most destroyed freedoms of individuals. Bailey's book was never referred to by the Y2K historians. I think he made a fatal admission in his second chapter. He indicated that since 1966 he had voted for presidential candidates of one party five times and the other party six times. He certainly failed the historians' "litmus test" of qualifications for rating our leaders. He simply was not a yellow-dog Democrat. Unfortunately, Bailey succumbs to the historians' premise that presidents can be ranked, and he too engages in the exercise.

The polls and the discussions and not just media exercises, they are fodder for our schools to use to brain-wash the public. Criticism of the efforts (whether Schlesinger's or Bailey's) is essential. One president does not have to be better than another. They are not in a tournament. In fact one, William Howard Taft, refused to participate in a survey of the greatest Americans taken in the 1920s. Enough cultism. We are a civic culture, and our number one virtue should be truth, and this "number one" game has been played outside of the boundaries of truth long enough.

TP, January 26, 2000

William N. Thompson

17. Tricks and Stones: On Nixon's Foul Mouth

New Nixon tapes have been released. We find again that in private conversations (though my Democrat friends would be quick to add that there can be nothing private in the People's Oval Office) Nixon had a foul mouth that delivered ethnic slurs. Again I must reflect upon my decency. I did vote for this man twice. Is something wrong with my soul? Is Richard Nixon's dirty mouth the measure of the man, his supporters, his party?

I was on the planning committee for a southwestern Michigan Republican picnic gala. Our featured speaker was Secretary of Agriculture Earl Butz. Tickets sales were not exactly going well. No one objected to the speaker. The trouble was it was mid-Summer 1974. Republicans were not in a gala-mood as we watched Watergate march toward its inevitable end. When it looked like we might keep the financial side of the gala to a small loss, Secretary Butz dropped the bomb on us. He would fly to Kalamazoo only in a private jet. Price tag—$2500. Butz refused to fly commercial. He came, and we ate the big loss. I did not appreciate this as I have never even flown first class. The next year I understood. Butz did fly commercial. Remarkably, Watergate "snitch" (was he the Linda Tripp of his day?) John Dean was seated near Butz. In a public fuselage 37,000 feet above the ground, Earl Butz was in a private conversation. He was asked why African Americans were not attracted to Republicans. His reply suggested they were interested in other things. The comments were a stereotyping ethnic slur. Dean wasn't using a telephone as he listened in, so he felt no state law would be broken if he repeated Butz' words to the press. President Ford had to confront Butz as the press gave no options. Butz resigned. A decade later, Secretary of the Interior James Watts referred to a physically-challenged person who had been appointed to a federal board with another word. After his press bashing, he resigned from the Reagan cabinet.

Loose lips sinks ships, loose lips cause cabinet members to lose their jobs. Past associations also cause others to be denied positions. One of Richard Nixon's supreme court nominees was discarded because he had been a member of a club that was racially exclusive. Loose lips of people standing next to Republican candidates can also cause them to lose their elections. In 1884, as Republican presidential candidate James G. Blaine was being introduced for a speech in the latter days of his contest with Democrat Grover Cleveland, he may not have been paying attention. In any event, after the introduction, Blaine simply got up and made his speech. He neglected to disagreed with the remarks of the one who introduced him, nor did he repudiate ethnic slurs the speaker made. The speaker had called Democrats the party of "Rum, Romanism, and Rebellion." "Romanism" was considered a slur against Catholics. Blaine was crucified in the New York City press and he lost a close vote in New York State. This loss gave the victory to Cleveland.

Vice President Dan Quayle was elected in 1988, but ever since that campaign began he has been bashed by the press for very innocent (certainly not malicious) misstatements that were most often off-hand comments in informal situations. The bashing precluded his opportunity to receive any hearing at all during an abortive presidential campaign this year. Candidate George W. Bush has repeatedly had his potential foreign policy ability and knowledge questioned by a press and opposition because he mixed up Slovenia and Slovakia in a speech. Both are new countries and small countries located far away.

Sometimes Republicans survive their sloppy mouths. Reagan did offer a "P" "joke" during the 1980 campaign, and after being panned by the press, he was able to put it behind. In "good humor" but with lousy judgement Vice President Spiro Agnew referred to a newspaper friend of his as a "Fat J-word" in a setting where many reporters were gathered. The reporter had Asian heritage. Agnew took a press beating, but the matter retreated into the background of the 1968 campaign.

How are Democrats treated? Well, sometimes they are forced out of office too. One Clinton cabinet member had to leave office for recommending that masturbation was a sexual option that should be taught to younger people. Our young president didn't like the onslaught of press attention on the matter—or maybe he didn't like the recommendation—and Ms. Elder was history. But what about Democrats who have operated at the top level? In the mid-1960s former President Harry S Truman (that's the one that is going to go down in the history books....you know...) called Martin Luther King Jr. a —-we'll as we are taught to delicately put it unless we are F.Lee Bailey or Warren Beatty—- "N-word." When reminded that King had won the Noble Peace Prize, Truman replied, "I didn't give it to him." The history books? McCullough finds it unworthy of mention; but McCullough does mention that Truman actually PAID membership dues to join the Ku Klux Klan in 1922, but withdrew his "application" before joining, because he found the KKK "also" hated Catholics—and Truman didn't like that as he had served with Catholics during the War. (He evidently hadn't served with African Americans or Jewish people).

Vice President Gore can say one inane stupid thing after another and it matters little to the press. One I like that I didn't see in print: in his first presidential announcement speech he affirmed that "I will not let the American people fend for themselves." Thank you daddy Al. His other stupidities rank with those of his predecessor, but they are glossed over. Today we still hear more about spelling "potatoe" than about Gore's arrogant ignorance.

Then there is our Commander in Chief. Once in Detroit he spoke to autoworkers. He too was introduced. One of his brain trusts from the labor movement told the crowd that they needed Clinton, that with Clinton those "J-word" (people) would not take their jobs away. Clinton merely thanked the labor "leader" for the introduction and started lambasting Republicans. I heard the introduction on C-SPAN, it never appeared in the press. No newspaper felt a necessity to spread the lack of repudiation of the racial slur to all the Asian-American voters and Asian residents in the land.

Clinton can make his stupidities ring out in public also, with little fear of being called on them. On October 8, 1999, Clinton made a speech in Ottawa, the capital city of Canada. He confused Quebec with France (these are not far away entities that were given their existence just yesterday—Quebec has been around since 1606, and France maybe a few years longer), then he spoke about the peace process in northern Ireland. He told the crowd about his Irish heritage (maybe he has discovered a lost great-grandfather in recent days). He mentioned difficulties of keeping peace. "It was like getting two DRUNKS to come out of tavern, and after all the trouble of getting them out, the drunks just turn around and go back in." I have Irish heritage too, and feel that there was an implied slur—hell no, it was explicit—and it was very public and international. While Clinton apologized, according to a television reporter, and did receive some appropriate bashing by the press, the incident was not covered by all daily newspapers—not in the Associated Press account of the speech in the <u>Las Vegas Review Journal</u>.

I guess I am bothered because my side has been denied the pleasure of seeing leading Democrats squirming and squealing as they are publicly reprimanded for being bigots, because the press is reluctant to expose them. I think I am bothered by the fact that Democrats say unacceptable things in public and suffer little, while Republicans are trashed for their private speech. But I am more upset at the press and others who howl "bigot" and "stupid" only when certain officials say unwise, stupid things, but not when others do the same thing—or worse. Most of all, I am bothered by those who feel that the measure of leaders is to be found in slips of the tongue, or in talk that is fully intended to be private. If the Nixon recorded remarks were on the telephone would the Democrats be howling, or would they take a Linda Tripp-posture and condemn the persons making invasive intrusions upon conversations? Nixon's offensive remarks were offered in private, even if they were recorded. If Nixon had used ethnic epitaphs or slurs in his bedroom conversations with Pat (if they were ever in the same bedroom), would critics howl at Nixon, or would they howl about invading the privacy of their private bedroom(s).

The press must stop playing the racial card in their game of "gotcha" unless the offensive remarks are offered in public or are delivered in some way to suggest a bigotry that intrudes upon policy making.

History professors have been very willing to overlook overt racism of Woodrow Wilson, perhaps believing that his League of Nation ideals supersede bigotry. Historians overlook the racism of a Theodore Roosevelt that led to murders of Filipinos by Americans during an insurrection. Bigotry was superseded by Teddy's bold character and domestic policies. Historians don't condemn presidents from Jefferson and Jackson through Lincoln, Wilson, and Truman for offensive patronizing (and public) words about Native Americans: "savages" "uncivilized," "barbarous," and "my children" (adult Native Americans were called "my children" in speeches by both Jefferson and Wilson). I love Truman's descriptions of when his grandmother "routed a whole band of Indians" by herself and her two shepherd dogs, "and they didn't come back and bother her anymore." I don't think that bashing of Truman for the words is appropriate. (The condemnation should be reserved for his policies of "termination" of Native tribal organizations). Nor is condemnation appropriate which is based simply upon a president's past associations (we are sensitive to things like this here in Las Vegas). Every president (including Clinton—query, were there female Rhodes Scholars in the 1960s?-ah that's right, women didn't have to be, the draft didn't cover them) has at sometime been a member of a group that excluded people of other races or genders. The mark of the leader should be results and public expressions that have public implications. It is appropriate that Truman be credited for desegregating the Military in 1948 (although we can ask why he waited three years?), and this is more important than a racist indiscretion in his young adulthood. Times change certainly, but the more important thing is that people individually do grow and change. A slave-runner grew up, repented, and became the composer of "Amazing Grace." Truman changed (maybe), I doubt if Wilson ever did.

In the case of Nixon, our judgements should point to his unacceptable behaviors regarding political corruption, and matters such as Detente with the Soviet Union and opening of a discourse with Communist China. In my case, I judge Richard Nixon for something else he did—something most Democrats opposed (and still do). I have two sons in their twenties. One is in college, the other is in the Peace Corps. My college-son is doing well but he is neither an all-A student nor Rhodes Scholar "material"; if there were a draft, he'd be fodder for the politicians. NIXON ENDED THE DRAFT! I will have absolutely no objection if my sons enter the military. I did so. Fortunately, I did not have to do Viet Nam. I am so so grateful that my sons will not HAVE to serve in any Viet Nam, in Kosovo, or Timor (or wherever Clinton's next war is) AGAINST THEIR WILL. In this singular move—ending the draft—Nixon gave more civil liberties to African Americans and Jewish people in this country than any Democrat has done as a result of his or her public policies; and the civil liberties gained—the personal freedoms gained—should certainly offset the words that flowed from his foul mouth in private conversations. We must judge not words alone but also deeds. Someone asked us to do that—I think it was Richard Nixon.

TP, October 18, 1999

18. Insinuations of Bigotry—Continuing

Well, it has started all over again. No Republican said a single word, yet the Chair of the Democratic Party has piped forth and the news media sheep have followed suit. The nomination of Democratic candidate for vice president has become a test of Republican bigotry. Will the Republican presidential win (if they don't blow it) be because of their appeals to bigotry—you know, like they tried in the 1960s?

Again the party of Abraham Lincoln, the Great Emancipator, the Grand Old Party that supported Union, and the 13th, 14th and 15th amendments (and brought my state Nevada into the Union as a political device to win approval of abolition) is on the defensive. The Democrats have so BOLDLY nominated a good man of a different faith for vice president, and so we have to prove our absence of bigotry by not opposing him. As a nominal Republican, I am sickened by the implications.

Now I have to be reminded of the bigotry that was used against John F. Kennedy. And I have to listen to his Houston Speech over and over again. And I begin to wonder if perhaps Kennedy used the speech on focus groups, or Kennedy used a polling outfit to check out the lines. Tucked into lines about how he will put the constitution above his faith he repeats a litany of issues where he will not let faith get in his way—birth control (I wouldn't think that one would), and gambling. Gambling was a faith issue for Catholics in 1960? I wish Kennedy were here so he could elaborate on that one. As I study the gambling issue, I find that contrary to Methodists and Baptists, Catholics have NO doctrinaire position on gambling. However, as a regular at the Sands, Kennedy evidently knew what he was talking about—or maybe he was throwing a bit of assurance to his Mafioso support base in the election (documented elsewhere).

The Republican Party is NOT the party of bigotry. There is no party of bigotry. If there was, it could be suggested that it is another party. Policies supporting bigotry in a public way were most strongly endorsed by another party—the party of the "solid south" the party that had to "balance" a Roosevelt with a Garner, a Stevenson with a Sparkman, a Kennedy with a Johnson.

The Jewish religion is a cornerstone of all Christian faith. As the Jewish faith is a faith of heritage, all Christians can make a claim to Judaism, as it is our heritage—OUR heritage. Indeed for centuries after the appearance of Christ on earth, many of his followers held to the belief that one had to be a practicing Jew before one could be a Christian. In my Protestant faith today, the Jewish heritage, the Jewish history, and the Jewish Law are primary elements—they are essential ingredients. More fundamentalist faiths embrace Israel and Zionism, they revere God's first covenant. They certainly do not reject Judaism, nor would they reject a person of Jewish faith today for political office. Compared to my Methodist religion, the Jewish faith causes me some confusion—a confusion shared I think with serious minded Jewish people. The "religion" is a religious faith, but it is also a place of history, and it is a feeling of heritage and community. How that history and heritage comes to work in individual lives is not exactly clear. (It is also unclear in most Christian faiths, but some have it down to the letter). There are rules and laws, yet in Judaism there is much debate over the rules and laws. From my observation, that is a beauty of Judaism. It is filled with intellectual vigor about competing interpretations and evolving interpretations of many of the rules. The religion spawns intellectual curiosity and active debate that I long for within the bland walls of my protestant tent. I would think that the best politicians would come out of Temple childhoods. There are many Judaisms, and I admire the diversity. Orthodoxy rejects seeking converts, and sees heritage of the community passing through the mother's line. On the other hand liberal Jewish thought accepts and even welcomes converts, and puts perhaps a greater emphasis on individual belief patterns.

Family is very important in my church, but my religion is not "inherited" in any genetic sense. It must be discovered each generation by each individual, although the mysteries of individual discovery are just that "mysteries." My grandparents were Baptists and Lutherans, my parents Presbyterian, myself a Methodist. No inheritance. Yet a person may be born "a Jew." Nonetheless that person is welcome anytime into my church, and may be transfer membership by letter—at least in some congregations. There is a rabbi and a synagogue, somewhere, that would welcome my transfer of membership as well if that were my serious intention. Yet. I still would not have the matrilineal heritage that gives other persons who are born Jewish certain rights, political rights such as eligibility for Israeli citizenship if they wish to avoid the consequences of legal processes in other jurisdictions.

I am still in a quandary as to why the Republicans have to suffer the awful collective label of bigotry because the Democrats nominated a good man of Jewish faith for political office. Was NOT the Republican Party the first party to nominate a Jewish man for a national ticket. Not for VICE president, but for president. Was not Barry Goldwater a man of Jewish heritage? Wouldn't serious students of Medellian genetics find that gene inheritance comes equally (or almost equally) through both father and mother? Certainly uni-gender Democrats would not categorize persons on the basis of what their mother's or father's race was. Would they hold it against Goldwater that it was his grandfather that was Jewish and not his grandmother? That would be quite SEXIST in our modern era, wouldn't it? Goldwater's belief system as a Christian incorporated Judaism, but then in Judaism, belief systems can at times be quite secondary. Had his heritage come through the grandmother, Goldwater could have become a citizen of Israel, regardless of the ingredients of his belief (assuming he did not reject his core Jewish beliefs, as other Christians also do not). The Republicans embraced a man with a Jewish heritage as their presidential candidate.

Perhaps the Republicans also nominated the first man of African American heritage—Warren Harding—for president. That is another story. But what should be noted is that a Republican President (Teddy Roosevelt) was the first to welcome African Americans as social guests in the White House, and that Harding was the first president of any religion or race to advocate full racial integration in American (he did so in a 1921 speech in Birmingham Alabama, for which he was roundly condemned by Democrats). The Republicans gave us our first Woman senator, our only African American senator of the modern era. And our vice presidential candidate's state gave us the first woman governor, and yes his state was the first to grant women the vote.

I am sick of people pointing fingers and yelling bigotry at groups. We all must look in the mirror first. I do, and I find much I don't like, and much I must atone for everyday. I am disgusted that one political party foists this issue on America. Their party chairman should have kept his fat mouth shut. His party is the one that calls for separation of church and state. His party is quickest to deny first amendment rights to people who wish to freely exercise religion in a public way. The bigotry in America toward religion is not toward the faith of the vice presidential candidate. Nor is it against Catholicism. A comedian would never get away with a religious joke or slur against these religions. But they sure get away with jokes against the unpolitically correct religions—Jehovah Witnesses, Mormons, and those whose faith is cast into disdain as being of the extreme "Religious Right." Funny, that the phrase "Religious Left" cannot be uttered today, isn't it? All of this reminds me of a word that my Liberal Democrat friends like to use a lot, especially when they are around Republicans. The word is "Hypocrite." I don't use the word. I just look in the mirror and see my personal imperfections.

TP, August 14, 2000

William N. Thompson

19. There's a Reason We Blow Up History in Las Vegas

Las Vegas, Nevada, is a very unlikely place to find American history. After all, in this city people worship the future as they always look to the next pull of a handle, roll or the dice, or deal of the deck; and also, they make a point out of forgetting that last loss. For those that do reach for history in Las Vegas, we thrown up little obstacles. Instead of making our historical sites entries on a national registry, we blow up the sites.

As the new national presidential campaign heats up (hopefully), Las Vegas will play its part. We have our own sets of temples that will be used by the fund raisers—both parties have made several pilgrimages already with hands out looking for alms for their poor candidates. In the future we may have to blow up another shrine to the almighty dollar lest we be found out. But today we can reflect on national politics by considering the shrines we blew up in the 1990s and what the bricks and rubble just might have been able to tell us if they could talk to us. Oh! Could they tell us some stories.

Now the ostensible reason we implode buildings in Las Vegas is that they are old—like maybe 40 years or so old—and we have to clear the way for progress. But I really suspect there is another reason. Let's consider three of the most famous recent implosions.

The shifting Sands of time, felled the Sands Casino in 1996. Today if you look for the Sands, all you see is an almost bigger than life replica of Venice, Italy complete with canals, shops, 3000 hotel rooms, convention center and a casino that makes the Lido Casino appear to be the size of a Manhattan candy store and bookie joint. But underneath the present day concrete structure there was a palace, "The" palace of Las Vegas in the late 1950s and 1960s.

The Sands was the home of "The Rat Pack" headed up by Frank "Ole Blue Eyes" Sinatra, Mr. Las Vegas himself, (a title later shared with Liberace, Elvis, and Wayne Newton, and maybe soon with Bill Clinton). Sinatra held court and everyone else danced for him, it was his stage and the rest of us were his jesters. Frank himself held a casino gambling license as he owned a Lake Tahoe casino and it was rumored that he held 9% of the Sands. He lost his license after he was challenged for entertaining and hosting Sam Giancana and a girlfriend (one of the McGwire Sisters). Sam was an "excluded person"—one of the most notorious organized crime figures that he was actually banned from all casinos by the state gaming control board. Rather than being contrite, paying a small fine, and promising not to do it again, Sinatra himself imploded with a string of vile invectives against Board members (some were recorded in telephone conversations), and he was out of gambling from 1963 into the 1980s.

Giancana was not only a pisano, he was part of the Sands legend, as he sent his girlfriend—a new one named Judy Campbell—to hang around with the "Pack." Peter Lawford was also part of the pack, and so also was a young senator, at least he was a hanger-on. The senator was actor Peter Lawford's brother in law, and he was seriously seeking the presidency. Sinatra and his mobster buddies saw an opportunity. The Washington political establishment was putting the heat on the Mob in various way including the activities of the McClellan Senate investigating committee. Maybe a new president could be persuaded to turn the heat down just a bit. The young senator was shmoozed and boozed, and he was fixed-up with Judy. he took her intimate friendship with him from the Las Vegas Sands right into the White House.

A couple problems arose out of this relationship. First, the Mob "thought" they had the new president bought (in addition to a girl friend they had bought him the key West Virginia primary—certainly with his daddy's knowledge), second, Mr. Sam Giancana and his close buddy Santos Trafficante had a contract from the Central Intelligence Agency to murder Fidel Castro. The Mob was anxious to reclaim its Havana Casinos, and the government thought that was the "Red, White, and Blue" thing to do. Two problems, one connection John F. Kennedy—Judy Campbell—Sam Giancana. Now the official word is that the appearance of Jack Ruby in Havana means nothing, the fact that Lee Harvey Oswald's surrogate father (uncle) worked for associates of Giancana (Carlos Marcellos Gang) in New Orleans, and that Ruby also did is all coincidental nonsense.

Okay for the official word. But just perhaps the skinny little ex-Marine didn't do "everything" by himself, then there could have been a very good Las Vegas Sands connection to an assassination of the president. Perhaps, a Castro retaliation, or perhaps a Mob hit because the President's brother attorney general Robert Kennedy kept up his pursuit of the Mob—he just couldn't back off a bit.

We also blew up the Landmark in 1995. We just had to expand the parking lot for the Convention Center. After all we get four million convention visitors a year, and what do they care about history. The "flying saucer atop a stick" shaped casino was purchased by Howard Hughes in 1968 before it opened. But alas Ramsey Clark and the Justice Team in the Johnson Administration felt Howard owned too much of Las Vegas—by now his purchases had given him about 30% of the Strip. Clark indicated he would not approve the purchase on anti-trust grounds. Hughes was furious, and he took out his sizeable pocketbook. He gave the Nixon for President campaign $100,000, and he had his right-hand man Robert Mahew give Hubert Humphrey a $50,000 bribe (the "little men" get less—or so it used to be).

So how could Hughes bribe Bobby Kennedy, also a presidential candidate? Not with money. Instead Hughes hired Larry O'Brien, Kennedy family bosom buddy, and postmaster general in the John F. Kennedy cabinet, to be on his legal staff. He was Hughes' lawyer at the time of the Nixon "contribution." Nixon was elected, Hughes bought, and then sold the Landmark (at least Nixon was a man of his word when he took the cash), and he departed Las Vegas as a very strange character. Trouble is, O'Brien became Democratic Party National Chairman in 1972 as Nixon prepared for his reelection campaign. Nixon panicked as he thought O'Brien had the "goods" on him, that O'Brien had solid evidence about the $100,000. Nixon's intelligence was incomplete. He never knew he held a checkmate, that O'Brien could not use the $100,000 bribe against Nixon, because Humphrey had also taken a bribe.

Nixon was not sure what O'Brien had, and what he might use regarding the Landmark deal. So a word or two to Erlichman and Halderman, another word passed down the line to Liddy, and soon the plans for the break-ins (many break-ins) were in place. Liddy's group was quite successful in its first attempts to compromise the offices of O'Brien in the Watergate complex in Washington, D.C., but alas in June 1972, they were caught. And the rest is "History." It is "Las Vegas History." The rationale for the Watergate break-in and the subsequent scandal that resulted in the first presidential resignation in U.S. History can be traced back to the corner of Paradise Road and Convention Center Drive in Las Vegas, and a parking lot where once the Landmark casino stood.

And then we blew up the Dunes in 1993. As the 2000 campaign gathers steam (if it ever gathers steam) the name Jimmy Hoffa arises once more. Actually the 25th year of his disappearance will be celebrated this month—on July 31. This year his son, also the president of the Teamster's Union, is a key player in the plans of Al Gore and Green Party candidate Ralph Nader. Which way will Hoffa Jr. throw his support. But the mystery lingers on—just what happened to Jimmy Hoffa, Sr. The mystery is not revealed. It is in the ashes and rubble of the Dunes, buried beneath the new super casino, the Bellagio, at Las Vegas Blvd. South and Flamingo Road.

Jimmy Hoffa financed the building of the Dunes with Teamster Pension Fund money. He loaned the money; the Teamster's got 2% on the loan (when banks were paying 5%), but Hoffa got an immediate 10% kickback, and Hoffa also got access to the casino cage where he was able to take a percentage of the profits in what we call a "skim" operation. (The "skim" was featured in the movie "Casino").

So it was in the early 1960s. But then, Bobby Kennedy kept up his crusade against Hoffa for misusing union money. One prosecution ended in a hung jury, but it was discovered that Hoffa had bribed a juror. In a new trial he was convicted of jury tampering, and sent to prison. He left Frank Fitzsimmons in charge of the union, feeling that Fitzsimmons would be loyal to him. Fitzsimmons was not loyal, and he cut Hoffa out of the information loop. While Hoffa rotted away in prison alone, Fitzsimmons kept up the skim operations, and kept the questionable "loans to casinos" going.

Hoffa was pardoned by Nixon in return for union support in the 1972 campaign. Actually Fitzsimmons arranged the pardon as a way Fitzsimmons could appear to be a friend to Hoffa who was still very popular with the truck driving membership of the union. However, Nixon and Fitzsimmons slipped a little one in on Hoffa. After Hoffa was released they forged the pardon to read that by accepting it Hoffa agreed not to participate in union activities until 1980. Fitzsimmons had guaranteed his own tenure in office until he would retire.

When Hoffa discovered this double-dealing trick he was furious, but he could not do much about it—until congress passed the Employee Retirement Income Security Act of 1974. Gerald Ford was president and William Usery was the secretary of labor. The Act gave the labor department new powers to investigate union pension corruption, and a task force was created to go after the Teamster's Union and Frank Fitzsimmons. The task force was able to get to Hoffa, and they reached an agreement. In exchange for solid information about how the loans to the Dunes worked, and how the Union participated in the "skimming" of casino profits, Hoffa would win a full pardon allowing him to take over union office whenever he was elected. The singing began, but the song hit a sour note on July 31, 1975. Jimmy Hoffa disappeared. Wanna bet his body lies beneath the Bellagio Casino and resort—probably below the nine acre lake and the fountains? It is what we do with history—bury it.

In Las Vegas we don't want history. History is about losers. We only want winners. And every loser can be a winner on the next roll, the next pull of a handle, or the next turn of a card—and that next event is in the future not the past.

HNN, July 9, 2001

Parables from (a not quite) Paradise, NV 89154

20. Like The District of Columbia Needs A(nother) Casino

Politicians are showing much better taste this year. They keep coming to Las Vegas for money. So much more class. Just four years ago the did their money grubbing in sacred houses of the Buddhist faith. Vegas already has its sleazy reputation—no pretensions about piety. I appreciate that our political party leaders come here rather than dirty the soil upon which holy people must walk. Vegas is a money grubbing place already. On the other hand, it is too bad that the party bag people have to fly all the way to Las Vegas. Such a waste of time and money, and also an interference with the activity of 33 million visitors who come to our city for legitimate reasons. (It's hard enough for them to get rooms without having to compete with blocs of party leaders). Wouldn't it be so much easier if there were a major casino property inside the beltway and the political money laundering could be done right at the seat of government—right at the point where the money is supposed to make a difference. Much more convenient.

Ironically, several District of Columbia local government leaders in the mid 1990s proposed that casino boats be docked within their jurisdiction. Imagine the concept. Congressmen, cabinet members, supreme court justices, maybe the president himself, could come to the casino and be wined and dined, then offered credit (loans) for gambling at the tables. Imagine lobbyists circulating within the facility the day before a major vote in congress or a major decision by the court. Imagine the opportunities to buy favors, to line the pockets of the mighty in exchange for policy outcomes. Imagine a gambling debt that goes uncollected, an unobserved gambling dealer paying off everyone at the table—even the "losers."

Well, you don't have to imagine. You only need to explore the history of Edward Pendleton (1790s-1858) and his "Palace of Fortune" located within walking distance of the houses of government in the District through the 1830s, 1840s and 1850s. The facility at 14th and Pennsylvania Avenue, North East, two blocks from the White House, became the favorite of the ruling classes. The nation's most important policy makers would wager at Pendleton's faro bank and dice tables, and inevitably lose. They would then become indebted to the casino owner (Pendleton). He, of course, was a lobbyist. Actually win or lose, he came out ahead. It is reported that in the 26 years he ran the "Palace of Fortune" he was responsible for the passage of hundreds of bills, most of which were private bills providing favors for selected citizens, at a big price.

The casino was also the meeting place where abolitionists and slave-owning senators could come together on neutral ground.

Many of the compromises that kept the Civil War from erupting until 1861 (or, on the other hand, made the War inevitable) may have been reached over the tables of the "Palace." James Buchanan was a regular at the faro bank, while a cabinet member and also while he was president.

Pendleton married the daughter of one of the leading city architects of the District. They became a dominant part of the social scene, well respected as many other gamblers are not in other venues. When Edward Pendleton died in 1858, his funeral was attended by the president and most leaders of congress.

If we could have just such a meeting hall in Washington, D.C., our politics could be so centralized. The money could exchange hands in one place—instead of the many casinos of Nevada or the other 25 casino states. Imagine that if the "Palace of Fortune" would have been open in Clinton's first term, the secretary of agriculture would not have had to go to the Super Bowl and fight the crowds in order to be with his most important "clients." He could have gone to the Capital Casino's sports book, and met his friends there. Also it would be so much more cooth to simply hand a congressman some chips rather than trying to slip him a briefcase full of money. Also, it would be an appropriate place for public leaders to become intoxicated, and it would have been a much more appropriate place to meet friends of the opposite gender (or same if that be the inclination) than among their younger staff members and interns.

Moreover if today there were a "Palace of Fortune" or a Capital Casino somewhere between the White House and Capital Hill, there would be a good place for defeated office holders to go for jobs. I would be much more comfortable thinking of my defeated congressman (or ex-cabinet member) as a dealer, or better yet for him or her, a valet parking cars, or becoming a professional shill, than having him or her accepting big salaries for merely linking their former official colleagues together with big rich interests. Casinos do provide good entry level jobs for many people who lack essential job skills. Indeed, Las Vegas is America's "Workfare" miracle. A District of Columbia Casino: it is like our liberal friends are wont to say "an idea who's time has come.!"

TP, July 26, 2000

William N. Thompson

21. The Government Can't Fill the Potholes, But It Can Gives Us Powerball? Dah!.

Wow! Powerball fever. Mass traffic jams on freeways into Connecticut and Arizona. Nothing like it ever before. Get real. Mass hysteria is nothing new. Cases of collective panic behavior have been well documented and analyzed by social psychologists for quite some time. Studies have shown that Orson Welles' radio drama, "Invasion from Mars," reached six million listeners in 1938 and induced panic activity on over one million people. When the truth was revealed, people cried out that the government should not allow such programs. Economic studies reveal how tulipmania dominated Holland between 1634 and 1637. Tulips were newly imported from Turkey and they became the "rage." So investors bid for bulbs and future crops, and the price just kept going up, up, up. Soon trading activity gripped the entire financial community as investors paid totally absurd amounts for a single tulip bulb. Some paid the price of a house in the hopes that the next person would purchase the bulb from them for even more. Then the bubble burst, fortunes were lost, and the government moved in to regulate market speculation on commodities and other investments. Other studies have assessed rampant fears that the king's armies were attacking civilians in France in 1789; only government action could slow the mania. And there have been mass contagions of anxiety about rumors of devil babies, doctors spreading poison gases, and witches spreading diseases. Again, as the panics set in, the public looked to their public leaders for answers.

So it appears that Powerball-mania has its precedents. And given the past, why would we expect any different behavior from a public, after all, now we have radio, television, newspapers and even cable television networks (and e-networks) spreading the news—there is a third of a billion dollars out there to be grabbed. All it takes is a one dollar ticket. The trouble is that this time there is no government that can protect us from the panic. THE GOVERNMENT IS CAUSING THE PANIC. The panic of Powerball-mania is the result of the natural advancement of marketing of state government lottery programs in our post modern computer age. If we love what we have seen our fellow citizens going through over the past month, great, because more is sure to come.

It was one thing to have a private stock exchange playing pyramid games with tulips, it was one thing to have a clever actor scare listeners of a radio show, it is quite something else to have governments spending one billion dollars a year to advertise and promote lottery games that put the collective population of our land into a panic. Is this what government is about? Is this what Jefferson meant when he said "that government is best which governs least?" When Henry Clay proclaimed that "Government is a trust, and the officers of government are trustees?" Lincoln offered that government exists to do those necessary things that the people cannot do for themselves. Rufus Choate told us that "The final end of government is to do good." Is this what governments are doing by having lotteries—doing good, doing necessary things we can't do for ourselves, governing only where necessary, exercising the public trust? Ah! But one may suggest, "the government is giving us a bit of happiness with our lotteries." This the purpose of government? NOT! I agree with William Ellery Channing who wrote "The office of government is not to confer happiness (upon the people), but to give opportunity to work out happiness for themselves" (Note: Quotations are from <u>Bartletts' Quotations</u>).

Powerball and other lottery games have as their purpose the creation of super millionaires. Is this the purpose of government to elevate by the laws of chance certain people among us to be super millionaires? To become super millionaires without doing one solitary productive activity. It is quite bothersome that among us there is one party that rails against "the rich." One party that sees all politics as a pitched battle between "the rich" and the "poor." And of course, that party speaks for the poor. Yet that is the party that tells us that we must fund government by having orgies such as our recent Powerball experience. In the last round of elections that party elected two governors (in Alabama and South Carolina) specifically and almost solely on the platform that they would bring a lottery to their states.

And that party keeps telling me that "W" only favors the rich with tax cuts, but "Oh where is his compassion for the poor."

The support of the Democrats for the lottery is a disconnect. I can understand why some Republicans also support the lottery—they are at least consistent as the lottery takes money from the poor and gives it to the rich—the new super millionaire winners, the large corporations that manufacture the tickets and then get a healthy commission for selling the tickets, and the beneficiaries of programs supported by lottery revenues. I sure can't suggest that the Democrats are Marxist on this one. Marx was against gambling because it was an activity of the idle rich, an activity that was non-productive, and an activity when placed in front of the poor was exploitive. Indeed, not only is lottery gambling non-productive, it wastes productive energies as it saps resources in its otherwise sterile money exchange. Outside of the exchange of ticket prices for prizes and government revenues it wastes over one billion dollars in promotions—one billion that could go to much better uses in society.

Contrary to what some may like us to believe no lottery ever created money, every lottery operates by taking existing money away from people. To elaborate: the lottery as a government fund-raising mechanism constitutes a very regressive tax. Study after study shows that poor people buy more tickets than others (per capita) and that the purchases represent a much bigger share of their wealth than the wealth of more affluent ticket purchasers. States purposely put sales outlets into poor neighborhoods. Lottery officials offer excuses such as "well they are the best customers," or "that's where the gas stations are."

The lottery officials also remind us that Jefferson—who vacilated considerably on the issue—did call lotteries "a painless tax, only paid by the willing." When governments spend over one billion dollars a year (3%+ of $38 billion in ticket sales) to advertise and push their product, I dissent to the notion that all purchases are "voluntary." I also dissent to the notion that the people (poor or rich) "demand" the lottery when lottery products utilize one billion dollars to do their "Vance Packard" sales gimmicks to suck in the customers.

The winners are not poor. But, say the lottery advocates, money goes for good causes—typically for education, and in the most innovative lottery state—Georgia—for college scholarships. Again, it is exploitation of the poor to benefit the affluent. Georgia college lottery scholarships go only to B average (high school) students and these include rich and poor alike. But to get a scholarship, the student must show that he or she CANNOT get a federal scholarship (Pell Grant, etc.). Georgia isn't stupid, it still wants those federal dollars. Who can't get the federal scholarships—those who cannot show need—the affluent. Who gets the lottery scholarships: a disproportionate share go to the affluent. Money also goes to K-12 schools to buy computers (The Al Gore solution to the education crisis). Computer companies raise prices (supply and demand, you know), and more rich people benefit. By the way, the schools do not have trained staff to utilize all the equipment and teach computer skills to the children.

But the lottery supporters suggest, how else can a poor person make it in society? The lottery is the only answer. Hogwash.

The lottery's implicit message that "this is the way to get ahead" is ironically the most anti-education message in society today, and the government is using one billion dollars to send the message out. Imagine instead of this message we had one billion dollars telling young people: "be literate, stay in school, graduate from high school, go to college." That's the formula to get ahead. Nine of ten who follow that formula will get jobs that will support them for life ("teach a person to fish..."), and in Las Vegas we call nine of ten, "a sure thing" like Tyson versus Butterbean. And five of the ten will become affluent with the formula, and one in ten will become rich (ergo have a six figure income). The recent powerball lottery gave the poor person a one in eighty million shot—not exactly your sure thing odds.

But where if not the lottery can the poor get money for college? Take the average regular lottery player. He or she spends $250 a year on tickets (more in the District of Columbia). Instead if a couple put $500 a year aside in a college fund for 20 years (I know this means delayed gratifications and it's tricky pushing religion), they would have enough money to pay the tuition of three children for four year degrees at public colleges and universities. And this is not gambling. Powerball-mania, madness, panic, or whatever you called it: for the public interest, it is powerball stupidity, and governments should not be in this business. Better they stick to what we need, better medical care, and filled potholes in our roads.

HNN, August 27, 2001

22. If Gambling Entrepreneurs Took Their Product to the F.D.A.

The compulsive gambler's prayer: "Please God, tonight let me break even. I really need the money."

American politics is dedicated to a central principle: the non-decision is sacrosanct, baring compelling evidence otherwise, the status quo shall be preserved. Thus, as in the "Ideal Type" legal rational bureaucracy described a hundred years ago by sociologist Max Weber, precedence has priority. Whether good or bad regarding particular matters, there is an overall aura of functionality in this principle. It allows all of us to go about our lives and our routines and plan for our mundane futures with some assurance that the rules of the game will not be changed on us mid-stream. We can accept a continuation of what we don't like with a resignation and a rationalization that "the devil we know" may be much better than the "devil we do not know." Hence, if the food and drug administration has decreed that a substance is forbidden, i. e. the chemicals in marijuana, it remains forbidden. If they have approved another substance that may be harmful (at least if given in massive doses to Canadian mice), that substance, nonetheless, may remain on the open market. Accordingly, sugar and fatty foods remain on very open market shelves even though they are known to be very harmful for sizeable portions of the population. It might be interesting to ask just "what if" they were not "grandfathered-in," what kind of restrictions might be put on their use.

So too, another product seems to be allowed on the open market shelf with but few restrictions. That product just may have a chemical substance attached to its use. Here, I pose the question: what if the FDA were given "gambling" and asked to approve its use for a consuming society.

On December 10, 1984 Thomas R. O'Brien, director of the new jersey division of gaming enforcement spoke to a meeting of the Sixth National Conference on Gambling and Risk Taking at Bally's Casino Hotel in Atlantic City. He commented:

"It seems to some of us, such a long time ago, that New Jersey undertook to establish this new industry as a 'unique tool of urban redevelopment,' the success of which is based upon how successfully that industry marketed its only product. That product is not entertainment or recreation or leisure—it's really Adrenalin—a biological substance capable of producing excitement—highs and generated usually by anticipation or expectation of a future event especially when the outcome of that event is in doubt."

"I think most of us here today who have had experience with gambling will agree that no form of risk taking or risk acceptance generates the intensity or can produce the amount of Adrenalin in the shortest period of time than a roll of the dice, spin of the wheel or turning of a card, and interestingly enough, the level of excitement is not in proportion to the amount of money riding on the event but depends to a large extent upon the subjective psychological approach to the game by the player."

The product of gambling, according to a top regulator was a chemical substance that while internally generated, still existed as a real substance in the body, and the substance moved to the brain and could affect mental activity, i. e. produce excitement and other feelings.

Let us ask if we would really legalize gambling if government officials accepted that gambling was in essence a mind altering drug—as Thomas O'Brien clearly suggested it was. Consider that legislators might have a hard time making such a decision. After all, how many legislators are biochemists? How many are pharmacologists? How many are medical researchers? None—or at least very few. As collective bodies legislatures lack the required expertise to make good decisions in the area of legalizing drugs.

Rather than flying blind, congress has another procedure. congress delegates authority to the food and drug administration.

So if FDA was given the mind altering "gambling drug" to analyze, would they legalize it? The answer is not easy. But the process they would follow in making a decision is clear. First, they would authorize extensive tests—initially on animals (perhaps those Canadian mice), but then on selected human beings. What would the tests tell them: Look at the 1000 who were asked if they had serious problem gambling symptoms (the DSM-IV Criteria established by the American Psychiatric Association) in a random population survey which I helped conduct a few years ago in Wisconsin. Of the 1000 surveyed, 12.9% had at least one symptom; of those indicating that they gambled, 19.8% had one symptom. Conclusion: perhaps the gambling drug is completely safe for 80.2% of those taking it. But 19.8% show one or more side effects that might be troublesome for them. Almost one percent of the population, and 1.4% of the users (in the Wisconsin study) exhibited several serious side effects. Using the psychiatric criteria we could suggest that these were serious problem gamblers—others might use the term "pathological" gamblers. These side effects could be potentially life threatening, as this drug leads to widespread urges to commit suicide. It also leads to socially unacceptable activities—stealing, writing bad checks, cheating on insurance matters, missing work regularly, family break-ups. From several surveys we discerned that between 20% and 30% of persons who are diagnosed (admittedly a process that has subjective attributes) as pathological gamblers actually admit that they have attempted suicide. No other group of addicted persons experiences such desperation with anything near as high a frequency.

The pathological gambler imposes hurt not only onto himself or herself, but also onto family members, friends, co-workers, those with whom he or she has business relationships, and onto the general public as well. It has been estimated that between 10 and 15 persons are directly and adversely affected by this person. The gambler will borrow from close associates, the gambler very likely will also steal. And when the associates can't pick up the pieces, the entire society may have to pay for welfare, for treatment costs, for police service, for jails and prisons. Conservative research suggests that each active pathological gambler burdens society (other people not in the family) with costs close to $10,000 a year.

But then this begs the question, after all, the drug does not seem to harm 80% of the users. In fact many of these might claim that the act of gambling—the "drug"—helps them relax, allows them to get away from daily work or home problems, gives them a measure of excitement lacking in other phases of their lives. They believe the drug improves their lives. Moreover, there may be economic advantages for promoting the commerce entailed in merchandizing the drug. Drug manufacturers (lotteries, casinos) provide jobs to society and the sales people pay good taxes. There is also evidence that some people will use the drug even if it is not legalized, and if they do, the government will not receive any taxes, nor will the government have the opportunity to control facets of how the drug is used.

So should such a drug be legalized? Perhaps. But before certifying any drug as safe enough to be legalized, the FDA would insist that certain controls be imposed. First, the FDA might recognize the gambling drug as an adult drug. They might stipulate that the drug could not be taken by children. The drug might be conditionally approved to be sold only in select locations and the dosages would be regulated. The buyers, moreover, might have to receive the prior approval of an outside expert (a doctor, perhaps, or in this case, a financial advisor, or a family counselor) before they could make a purchase. And experts (again, doctors, or financial advisors) might have to monitor the drug use and certify that the individual taking the drug was not having serious side effects. When the side effects became noticeable, the person would be weaned off the drug, or in serious cases taken off the drug immediately and completely, lest the drug become addictive.

The FDA has established elaborate controls for the dispensing of drugs. Government policy makers might be wise to follow FDA-type procedures as they establish additional controls over gambling in order to assure that serious problem gamblers do not succumb to the bad side effects of what might otherwise be a good drug for many people. Certainly policy makers should consider the FDA analogy before they legalize more of the drug.

HNN, October 29, 2001

William N. Thompson

23. A Childhood Thought of a Lucky Las Vegas Resident

The cub scout troops of Eberbach Elementary School held their annual carnival on the playground one April Saturday afternoon. As I recall I was about nine years old. I lived four blocks away. That afternoon I was riding my bicycle around with little to do. I had fifteen or twenty cents in my pocket. I rode by the school and saw the carnival and I decided to walk around the playground. As I went down the "midway," I discovered a game I had never played before. People were pitching pennies onto an oil cloth that was marked in a grid with 100 squares. Each square had a number or an "x". The numbers were one, five, ten, and 25. If a penny landed on a square, the person pitching the penny won the amount of pennies designated—but the penny could not be on a line, it had to land fully within the square.

I remember making several pitches and winning five or ten cents. I eagerly waited my turn to throw one penny after another. Soon I was out of pennies, but I was quite charged up. I looked all about for another penny, on the ground, in my pockets. I turned each pocket inside out. Then I ran to my bicycle and pedaled home as fast as I could. I ran about the house looking for loose change. I found another ten cents in a dresser drawer and quickly rode my bicycle back to the carnival. I ran to the penny pitch booth. I started throwing pennies again, and again they missed the mark and my pockets were emptied. I thought about riding home again, but I knew it would be too late, the carnival was already beginning to close down. I saw a friend and begged him to loan me money. He just laughed at me. I was very very dejected as I rode home. All night long I woke up thinking of the penny pitch game.

Thirty-one years later I moved to Las Vegas. Here I have been much luckier than when I was nine years old. Here, in my very first gambling experience, I lost. Although I only gamble on semi-rare occasions, I almost always lose. After I return home, I feel no rush to gamble. I felt it once, and I think I could have the feeling again, but I have been very very lucky, almost every time I gamble now, I lose. And I know I am a loser. Sometimes I think that is the only way one can really survive in Las Vegas.

(A Random Thought)

24. Abolish The Office of Attorney General

It's 1974....

Our nation has been rocked by a series of events, which suggest corruption in high circles of government. Many of the events have involved the office of United States attorney general.

First, it was revealed that former Atty. Gen. John Mitchell had failed to pursue criminal prosecutions of certain persons who had contributed heavily to a national political campaign which he directed. Mitchell and former commerce secretary Maurice Stans are on trial now in New York on charges growing out of their roles in President Nixon's political campaign of 1972.

Second, Atty. Gen. Richard Kleindienst, Mitchell's successor, resigned because his personal friends were implicated in the Watergate case, and he feared a conflict-of-interest in any prosecution. Then L. Patrick Gray, the acting FBI director (a position under the attorney general) failed to win senate confirmation as permanent director and resigned because he had destroyed evidence about the Watergate scandal.

Subsequently, Atty. Gen. Elliot Richardson, Kleindienst's successor, resigned because the President demanded that he fire Archibald Cox, the special Watergate prosecutor Richardson had chosen. Richardson's successor now is William Saxbe, who was a Republican senator from Ohio prior to Mr. Nixon's appointment of him as attorney general.

Independence

Some observers of this most bizarre chain of events have begun to ask some pertinent questions concerning the office of attorney general. For instance, just what is the function of this office in our political system? Whom does the attorney general represent?

To whom should he be responsible? Should he be independent of partisan political pressures? Such questions no doubt imply that something is not acceptable with the present arrangements. This writer would agree. In this article it will be argued that the questions asked are really not difficult ones. Quite simply, they do not have to be answered. The office of attorney general of the United States, instead, should, be abolished.

The present day department of justice, headed by the attorney general, supervises the work of 92 federal district attorneys in the prosecution of persons accused of breaking federal laws. In such a role the attorney general can encourage certain kinds of prosecutions, and he can also exert influence to hinder prosecutions. Through its component FBI and the internal security division, the department of justice is empowered to render a wide range of investigative activities which reach into the personal lives of many American citizens, law abiding and otherwise. Moreover, the attorney general oversees the federal prison system, and the process of federal pardons and parole.

Many of the attorney general's duties, however, are not in the realm of criminal law. He heads an antitrust division which seeks to keep American business enterprises free and competitive, a civil rights division which seeks to enforce antidiscrimination legislation and court policy, and a tax division which providers legal services when it becomes involved in litigation. The tax division also prosecutes violators of the tax law. The department of justice also contains a Civil Division, a land division, Immigration Services, and solicitor general's office.

It can be seen that, the attorney general performs two kinds of duties. He serves as the chief law enforcement officer of our nation, guarding it against internal enemies, essentially those commit criminal acts. Secondly, he is the chief executive of an agency, which performs civil duties, many of which call for political policy decisions.

Is there not better way of running a department of justice than by having an attorney general appointed by a president and removable by a president at will? In his criminal law enforcement roles, should not the office be completely independent of all men? Yet how could we reconcile this independence with the policy-making roles of the office? Must not the attorney general also be in touch with political forces?

States Differ

Although there is no precedence at the federal level for any alternative to the current selection method, various alternatives have been tried in the states. In 42 states, the attorney general is popularly elected on a partisan ballot. Of these states, only Oregon designates that the election will be at a time different than the time of the governor's election. Six states (Alaska, Hawaii, Pennsylvania, New Hampshire, New Jersey, and Wyoming) provide for gubernatorial appointment. In five of these states, the Attorney General serves at the governor's pleasure. In New Hampshire, he serves a five-year term. This was the practice in New Jersey prior to 1947. The Maine legislature elects the attorney general, while in Tennessee he is selected to an eight year term by the state supreme court.

This writer has examined careers of 446 state attorneys general who served between 1930 and 1970. Comparisons between those who came to office by popular election and those that were appointed (either in the eight states, or in the other states to fill vacancies) revealed some items worthy of note. The 228 popularly elected were in some sense more political than the 158 appointees. In other senses they were more judicial in their behavior. Almost twice as many of the elected group held major party offices while they were attorney general. Thirty seven per cent of the elected group sought higher political offices (governorship, seats in congress) compared with only 19 percent of the appointees. Twice as many elected attorneys general moved onto positions as government administrators, while one and one half times as many appointees moved onto judicial posts.

Questionnaires received from available appointees showed that they has a greater inclination to serve government agencies, while the elected group was more likely to see their role as a servant of the people. This was confirmed in an analysis of opinions state attorneys general issued on race relations, criminal law, and church-state questions. In all three areas, the elected group of state attorneys general wrote opinions more consistent with United States supreme court decision. The appointees were more likely to resist new federal decisions. These facts suggest that a greater independence comes with popular election. They indicate that an attorney general who is not appointed by an executive will be less likely to see his tasks as that of representing the executive, but rather will see service of the general public as a more desirable role. Such a role could more easily permit investigations of wrongdoing by other government officials.

The data of my study did not indicate how politics could be taken out of the office; indeed it suggested that partisan politics was more likely to be a part of an elected attorney general's operation. Moreover, no solution was suggested by the data for the problem of wrongdoing by the attorney general himself.

Scoundrels

Regrettably, the office of attorney general in both state and national has attracted its share of scoundrels. Having the attorney general investigate corruption has at times been like putting the fox in charge of the chicken coop. Merely changing the office, from an appointive to an elected one, will not solve the problems posed. The way the federal office is currently constituted, it will not be able to perform adequately whether elected or appointed.

An executive needs an attorney if he is to be an effective policy leader for a government. It is a function of that attorney to serve the executive. But society also needs justice. The only way to achieve a proper balance between two forces inherent in the office would be to abolish the office altogether, and to assign its functions to other officials of the government. First of all, the criminal law functions of the office must be separated from political pressures, which are quite appropriate for civil law functions. A separate commission of criminal justice should be established. The commission should have jurisdiction over the FBI, Internal Security Division, federal corrections institutions, paroles, and the administration of pardons. All federal prosecutions should be under control of the commission. Federal district attorneys should be responsible to the commission in all their criminal law activity. The commission would be empowered to intervene in or actually initiate prosecutions at he district level.

Power Listed

The commission would be able to investigate all governmental activity to discern whether any acts of bribery, corruption, or violations of public trust have occurred. The commission would have full powers to investigate and subpoena all government officials. This commission must be totally divorced from partisan politics. It could consist of from one to three commissioners who would be appointed for either a 15-year term, or perhaps until they reach age 65 or 70. They would be permanently barred from holding any other government position or engaging in any partisan political behavior. The appointment would properly be made by the president with the confirmation of two-thirds of both house of congress. Acting commissioners could be appointed by the supreme court. Removal of a commissioner could be by impeachment or by an order of the supreme court after a full hearing. Application for such an order could be brought by any citizen, and processed in a manner similar to disarmament proceedings.

The title of attorney general would be worn by no individual. No continuity with past powers, practices, or personalities in the office of attorney general of any jurisdiction would be maintained. A new commission would not trace its origins to the likes of a Mitchell.

The civil law duties now performed by the department of justice would be assigned to the line agencies of the federal government. For instance, the naturalization and immigration division could be assigned to the state department. The land division to interior, and the anti-trust division to the federal trade commission. The tax division could be attached to the internal revenue service with all criminal activities prosecuted by attorneys for the commissioner of criminal justice.

Legal Services

Replacing the solicitor general could be an office of government legal services. This office could be attached to the executive office of the president. Its function would be to coordinate legal services between agencies and to set standards for civil litigation involving the federal government.

Powers Listed

The president would have political control over this office as he would in an indirect fashion over all civil legal services of the federal government. He would have no jurisdiction over criminal prosecutions.

While these suggestions probably do not answer all the critics of the present day office of attorney general, they would certainly go a long way toward making an unacceptable mixture of justice and politics into a rational division of legal authority. One set of lawyers could again follow only the doctrine that the law is above all men; while other government attorneys could direct their efforts towards the service of the policy goals of governmental actors.

*This essay first appeared in the Kalamazoo (Michigan) Gazette, April 9, 1974. The ideas have retained their merit over the past three decades during presidential administrations of Jimmy Carter, Ronald Reagan, George H. W. Bush, William Jefferson Clinton, and George W. Bush.

William N. Thompson

25. The Ironies of a Nuclear State

For the last 70 years, Nevada has been neither a Democrat state nor a Republican state. It has consistently been the gambling state. The voters—only a handful of whom have been born in the state, have tolerated—and voted for—both very liberal and very conservative candidates for state and federal office. Taking their cues from a gambling industry which invests heavily in political campaigns, the voters have never tolerated candidates who show independence or weakness vis-a-vis the real "party line," ergo, the full-fledged support of casino gambling, as determined by the casino industry.

But now the state has a new bottomline "critical issue." Now all aspiring politicians must rally around another cause as well. They must be willing to "go to the mat" to show that they oppose having nuclear waste brought to the state and put into a repository at Yucca Mountain, 100 miles northwest of Las Vegas. "No Nuclear Waste," and "Nevada is not a Wasteland," have become the battle cries of our public leaders and also of our populace.

There are many ironies regarding the new rigid stance taken by the state. The first irony concerns the vehemence with which the leaders and followers seek to protect "their" land, and the vehemence with which they cry out that "Nevada has already done its share," for the nation. What does "our" land mean, anyway? Not one of the five most recent governors of Nevada was born in the state. Only 6% of the adults of southern Nevada (Las Vegas and surrounding Clark County) were born in the state. Statewide, 13% of the population is native born, the smallest percentage among all 50 states. The average resident of southern Nevada came to the state (or was born in the state) in 1991. Yet majorities loudly protest that the waste which may be placed in "our" desert lands 100 miles away will destroy "our" quality of life, to say nothing about destroying the influx of tourist dollars to Las Vegas. We do get 36 million visitors per year.

Very few of the new residents, and almost none of the tourists has ever driven by the lands where the waste may be stored. The lands are miles away from the road running 450 miles to Carson City, Tahoe and Reno, and most people going that way fly. We are simply not familiar with "our" lands.

A second irony concerns the lands with which we are familiar—lands within the Las Vegas metropolitan area. Here we almost categorically refuse to take ownership over "quality of life" issues. There is almost zero political or public outcry about the many social maladies that beset us—high school drop out rates, teen age pregnancies and suicides, adult suicides, smoking and cancer deaths, drunk driving incidents, child abuse and child abuse deaths, myriad addictions including, of course, compulsive gambling. All these factors find Nevada among the nation's leaders (on the wrong side of the equation). Yet no casino dollar has been given to a candidate in order to make an appeal that might address these "problems" for "our" land. The nuclear waste issue also preempts concerns about the real crises of high malpractice insurance rates prompting doctors to leave Las Vegas, and also the minimal numbers of nurses in the state—the lowest number per capita in America. (Las Vegas Review Journal, February 24, 2001; March 6, 2002).

A third irony concerns the notion of "ownership" of the desert lands and the desires to keep the lands free of nuclear contaminants and the political history of the state. The actions of politicians (acting with public support) over the years since 1930 (around when full casino gambling was legalized throughout the state) belie concerns for a clean earth policy. The politicians and then-residents of the state eagerly sought out federal selection for a variety of military and defense projects including ones involving nuclear energy and nuclear weapons. Federal military-related programs are the second biggest sector of the state economy.

Hawthorne had 250 residents in 1920 and it was headed toward becoming another Nevada ghost town. However, a disaster at a New Jersey Navy ammunition depot presented an opportunity. U.S. Senator Tasker Oddie and Representative Samuel Arentz (both of

Nevada) persuaded the department of war to place a new ammunition facility in the dry desert terrain of Hawthorne. Now an Army ammunition site, the depot still provides the economic basis for the small city. (Hulse, The Silver State, 1991, pp. 333-5).

The Army Air Corps placed a training facility just north of Las Vegas in 1942. After World War Two state political leaders including the late Howard Cannon used their seniority to have Nellis Air Force Base made the essential jet flight training school as well as air gunnery (live fire) range for our military. Cannon also worked hard for the placement of an MX missile defense system in the state, but on that score he did not have universal support among the population, albeit many in Las Vegas were counting the dollars expected to come with a real estate boom and 100,000 new residents. Other air stations have been placed near Reno, in Fallon and at Wendover, on the Utah state border. (Hulse, pp.214-5, 271).

At the conclusion of World War Two a program of testing nuclear weapons began on several Pacific Ocean islands. However, logistics made planning and execution of the tests somewhat inconvenient. In 1950 President Truman secretly planned to move the tests to a site within the United States. A site adjacent to the Nellis gunnery range at Yucca Flats in the Nevada desert was selected. The first atmospheric bomb test was made on January 27, 1951. From then until atmospheric tests were finally stopped in December 1962 (and banned by a treaty in August 1963), over 100 bombs were dropped above the ground. Between 1963 and 1993 about 800 more tests were conducted underground. (In all there were 928 tests in Nevada). However, nuclear materials were vented into the atmosphere in at least 200 cases with underground tests, with some of these tests propelling nuclear particles off of the test site. (LeBaron, America's Nuclear Legacy, 1998, p. 70).

While the selection of the site was made in secret, it cannot be said that the decision was opposed by Nevadans. Powerful U. S. Senator Patrick McCarren supported the move entirely, as did residents who saw the Nevada Test Site as a great source of economic benefit for the state. UNLV Political Scientist A. C. (Dina) Titus wrote in her book Bombs in the Backyard (1986), "...the southern Nevada papers strongly endorsed the testing program, presenting the public with positive headlines and patriotic editorials....state officials at every level were eager to accommodate the needs of the new facility which brought in federal dollars." She added that press coverage "failed to address more serious questions about the possible harmful effects of fallout." (p. xiii).

Residents did not protest. Instead they held parties at the edge of the city from whence they could see the flash of a nuclear blast, and if they were "lucky" they could view the mushroom cloud. Indeed, a fiery nuclear cloud was the symbol found on the Clark County official seal in the 1950s. Casinos held promotional events tied to the explosions. In 1957, the Sands, home of the "Rat Pack," held a "Miss Atomic Bomb" contest with the winner decked out in a scantily-sized bathing suit which was shaped like a mushroom cloud. (Titus, p. 93).

The same year, according to Titus (p. 97), the Nevada state senate passed resolutions asking the federal government to "build an experimental nuclear-power generating plant" in the state, and also to use the Naval Ammunition Depot at Hawthorne to store "nonconventional weapons."

The residents downwind from the atmospheric tests, most of whom lived in Utah, were not as "lucky." Actually the American public has not been lucky. One federal study reveals that it is likely that nuclear weapons tests have caused at least 15,000 cancer deaths in the United States. (USA Today, February 28, 2002).

To be sure, the negative effects of the nuclear radiation were not fully addressed. Perhaps now the political establishment is making up for that early neglect with its rigid "no waste" policy. However, by the 1950s the effects of radiation poisoning were known, and certainly results of the atmospheric "tests" over Hiroshima and Nagasaki were rather public.

In 1984 when presidential candidate Gary Hart stated that he would seek a moratorium on underground testing, Nevada organized labor immediately attacked him. His Nevada campaign headquarters disavowed the stance. In 1992 state political leaders while already nearly unanimous in opposition to the placing of even low level nuclear waste in Nevada, stepped forth to protest the stopping of underground nuclear tests, and they lobbied hard to make sure the Test Site itself was not closed down. At its peak time of operations the Nevada Test Site facilities did provide employment (with support jobs) for over 18,000 Nevadans. (Titus, 68, 100).

Alas when underground tests were stopped, Nevada officials sought more nuclear projects for the state. In 1995, the state's two U.S. Senators, Harry Reid and Richard Bryan, both protested when Savannah River, South Carolina was selected over the Nevada Test Site to have a multi-billion dollar radioactive gas production plant. "This is one of the types of things that gives congress the bad name it now has," Reid opined. Bryan added, "This is abominable public policy." They claimed that Nevada lost the nuclear project because of "pork barreling." (LVRJ, August 5, 1995).

In 1996 the state's congressional delegation also protested when congress determined that tests at the site would be permanently banned. Senator Reid sought an amendment allowing the president to authorize a test on his own when he deemed it necessary. Reid was roundly criticized by Nevada environmentalists and groups such as Greenpeace for his actions seeking continued testing. (LVRJ, June 27, 1996).

As an aside, in November 1997, the Nevada legislature passed a resolution asking the Smithsonian Institute to return the Enola Gay, the plane from which the atomic bomb was dropped on Hiroshima, to Wendover, Nevada, where it was located before flying to Tinian Island and then Japan. The legislature thought it would be a wonderful exhibit to use to attract tourists to the desert town. Things we like to celebrate! No wonder Halloween is a state holiday. (LVRJ, November 14, 1997).

By the 1980s the nation had 78 Nuclear energy facilities. Waste materials were beginning to be amassed at each of the sites.

The waste is now stored in cooling ponds at the reactor sites. However if the ponds become filled, the waste will have to be in above the ground dry containers. The manner of storage in both cases is not totally secure. The waste materials are subject to weather disturbances (tornados and floods), as well as earthquakes and even volcanic eruptions. The events of September 11 also raise concerns that the multiplicity of sites would be more vulnerable to sabotage. That thinking was also present in 1982 when congress passed the Nuclear Waste Policy Act. The act provided for the creation of a waste storage site by 1998. The site would be paid for by taxes on the nuclear facilities. At first three potential sites would be selected and studied for feasibility. Then the president would pick one of the sites, after which the host state's governor could veto the plan. The veto could be overturned by majority votes in both houses of congress. Sites in Washington State and in Texas were studied along with Yucca Mountain, Nevada. However in a new action, Congress in 1987 passed an act that limited study to the single site at Yucca Mountain. Political leaders in Nevada called this law, not affectionately, the "Screw Nevada" Law. In 1989, the law was changed again, this time putting a date of 2010 for the opening of the waste facility. (Los Angeles Times, January 29, 1995).

In February (this year), President Bush selected Yucca Mountain to be the site. Nearly $7 billion had been spent in scientific and other studies of the site. Bush also indicated his choice was based upon concerns about terrorism at the scattered nuclear power facilities. Soon afterwards, Nevada Governor Kenny Guinn vetoed the plan. We now are awaiting action by congress. Congress has 90 days to override the veto. (LVRJ, February 16, 2002; New York Times, March 9, 2002).

Politics or Science? The answer has to be a simple one: Politics. There is no way to measure the terrorism factor with scientific accuracy. Placement of all waste at Yucca Mountain will afford great security. However, the risky question persists: is it better to keep nuclear waste at 78 power plants (and other military sites) in 39 states, or is it better to transport the materials thousands of miles through 42 states on its journeys to Nevada? Right now, the September 11 fear mentality seeks to reduce the number of major targets, and individual trucks or rail cars carrying waste are not viewed as major targets, albeit many precautions will be taken over the transportation routes.

The Nevada response points to scientific questions about possible long term (measured in hundreds or thousands of years) leakage of materials into water tables in the desert, and also to risks of transportation sabotage or accidents. However, the "group think" psychology of Nevada politics sees voters responding positively to rigid political positions against "all" nuclear waste materials. "Political" has to be the conclusion considering the continuing record of the state's support for nuclear testing activity. The same political leaders that are quick to point out how the state has already made its sacrifices (in having politically acceptable and economically beneficial military facilities and nuclear testing facilities), now point to great damage that will be done to the state, its reputation (?), and its citizens' health by having waste stored in the state. They have riled up a population that is quite blaze about social maladies in their neighborhoods to be quite angry about degradation of desert lands that a few years ago were the sites for atmospheric and underground nuclear blasts.

To be sure, this writer absolutely does not want nuclear trucks or rail cars moving through the populated Las Vegas metropolitan area. At the same time he would like to see some political concern for the social pollution and the impending medical services crisis in our populated communities as well. And that view, consistent with long standing views in Nevada politics, is neither Democrat nor Republican.

HNN, March 25, 2002

26. The Concept of Nullification—The Latest Round

The annals of federal state relationships have been punctuated by several episodes of state efforts to nullify federal executive actions. In the past these efforts have been essentially extra legal (and/or illegal), and they have been unsuccessful. A contemporary nullification fight—one going on at this very moment—is different. It is taking place under the guise of federal law according to procedures set down in words by the national congress. The effort will, however, end the same, it will fail.

The current effort of state nullification of federal executive action will, on the other hand, be a successful one if it wins support of a single house of congress. The processes of this nullification campaign are convoluted, to say the least. Whichever way the matter is concluded after congressional action, the fight will continue in federal courts with a constitutional challenge of those processes.

Today's nullification battle is the fourth such battle in our nation's constitutional history. The three previous fights included South Carolina's attempt to repudiate enforcement of federal tariff policy in 1832, the collective effort of eleven southern states to block federal enforcement of laws during the Civil War Era of 1861-1865, and the efforts of many of the same states to interpose their authority on behalf of their citizens against implementation of federal policies mandating racial integration of schools in the 1950s and 1960s.

The government of South Carolina was convinced that the 1828 and 1832 national tariff acts which called for high protective tariffs on manufactured goods were designed to assist northern industry to the strong detriment of their own agricultural interests. The acts were also seen as an attack upon the economic viability of the institution of slavery. Leaders in South Carolina protested the federal efforts by calling a state convention which passed resolutions indicating that the tariffs would not be imposed at ports of entry into the state. The strongly worded resolutions indicated the state would use force to support its cause.

President Andrew Jackson found that the state actions precluded any opportunity for compromise. Although he was a states' rights advocate and he was born in South Carolina, Jackson responded in kind. He mobilized troops and he ordered them to South Carolina if the state resisted implementation of the tariff provisions. congress supported his moves. South Carolina backed down. In the process, its leading politician, John C. Calhoun, resigned his position as vice president of the United States. In 1833, the Great Compromiser, Henry Clay, maneuvered a bill through Congress which made the episode less onerous for South Carolina. The state repealed its nullification proclamation. The 1833 tariff act gradually rolled back tariff rates to pre-1828 schedules.

The results of the next nullification episode were not as peaceful. In 1861 South Carolina nullified the constitution and all federal law enforcement in its borders. South Carolina was followed by ten other states, and the Civil War ensued. This failed case study in nullification is amply recorded in tens of thousands of books.

Post Civil War compromises on the enforcement of certain federal provisions (constitutional and statutory) in the states formerly in rebellion allowed the states to impose illegal (in effect, if not in word) policies of racial segregation in public facilities. The state policies mandating public separation of races were ruled unconstitutional in 1954 by the United States supreme court. The next year the court issued rulings regarding the immediate implementation of national policies for integration.

The governors of the states with policies of segregation began a pattern of resistance to the decisions. Supported by their state legislatures, governors such as Ross Barnett of Mississippi, Orval Faubus of Arkansas, and George Wallace of Alabama orchestrated the policy of interposition. The governors soon found themselves "standing in the school house door" blocking federal enforcement agents from accompanying African American students into previously all-white schools. At the school sites the governors would be flanked by the commanders of their state national guard along with troops of the guard. The guard would represent a show of force against federal action. But inevitably, it was but a show. As if by prearrangement, in each case the president would proclaim that the state national guard was to called into federal service and placed under command of the U.S. Army. The "Army" would in turn leave the governor's side and support the actions of the federal agents. Interposition and other legalistic efforts to resist policies of integration did slow down implementation, but national policy prevailed.

The fourth nullification episode is the first one to take place outside of the South. (An 1812 Hartford Convention advocated nullification, but this was a meeting of Federalist Party politicians not government officials). The current episode was prompted, the better word would be "created," by the Nuclear Waste Policy Act of 1982. The Act provided that the federal government (Department of Energy) would study sites for storing nuclear waste materials generated by power plants (and other facilities) in 42 states. After the study was completed, the secretary of energy would recommend one site for storing nuclear waste underground.

The president would then accept or reject the site. If the president agreed with the selection, he would inform the state where the site was located that he had made his selection. The governor of the state would then have 60 days in which to veto the action of the president. If there was no veto, action on developing the site would begin. However, if, as expected, the governor vetoed the president's action, the veto could be overridden only if both houses of congress voted to over ride (by majority vote) the veto within ninety days. If but one house supported the governor, the governor's veto of the president's action would be confirmed. The process of selecting a nuclear waste site would have to begin anew.

The 1982 Act also indicated that the department of energy would start its study by looking at sites in Texas, Washington State, and Nevada. In 1987, another act of congress limited the study of potential sites to the Yucca Mountain site in Nevada. On February 14,

2002, after fifteen years of study costing the federal government over 12 billion dollars, Secretary of Energy Spencer Abraham recommended the Yucca Mountain site for storage of nuclear waste. On February 15, 2002, President George W. Bush selected the Yucca Mountain site. As expected, on April 9, 2002, Nevada Governor Kenny Guinn vetoed the action of the president. This is the first time in American History that a governor has "legally" (I emphasize the quotation marks) vetoed the action of a president. Congress has until July 9, 2002, to sustain or override the veto.

The politics are quite simple. Nevada has four votes in congress, two in the House, two in the Senate. The forty plus states with nuclear waste within their borders (now temporarily stored above ground at the generating sites), have over 400 votes in the House and over 80 votes in the Senate. If they want to keep the waste at the temporary storage areas which are quickly filling up in many cases, they may vote to sustain Governor Guinn's veto. If they fear transporting the waste through their states toward Nevada more than they fear having the waste permanently in their midst, they may also sustain the veto. However, by sustaining the veto they are introducing the possibility of having another waste site, perhaps a site in their own state.

If they vote to override the veto, they are assured that most of the waste will be moved to Nevada (all of the waste will be moved over a timed schedule).

The congressional votes are being lobbied and counted. The nuclear energy generating plants and the power companies want the waste moved to Nevada and they have lobbying funds to support overriding Governor Guinn's veto. The state of Nevada has authorized the expenditure of three million dollars in their campaign to win congressional support for the veto.

Ironically, at the very moment the state of Nevada is waging its costly uphill battle for a nullification victory, the state's department of motor vehicles (DMV) is reconfirming the state's love of everything nuclear. (See March 25 HNN). On April 12, 2002, the

DMV announced that the state would be raising money by selling automobile license plates honoring the history of the Nevada atomic bomb testing site at Yucca Flats (adjacent to Yucca Mountain). The new state license plates actually show an atmospheric atomic bomb test. The plate has a mushroom cloud rising through the plate number and encompassing the word "Nevada." The cloud is flanked by a nuclear logo and the formula $e=mc2$. There are estimates that 15,000 Americans died as a result of the atmospheric tests. Nevada likes to talk about the danger of radiation. But the state just can't quite resist celebrating its nuclear past and making a buck off it in the process. I expect the license plates will be issued in time for Senators Reid and Ensign to sport them on their cars in Washington, D.C., as they drive about seeking votes to support Governor Guinn's veto.

The nullification fight will not end in July 2002. The veto arrangement with a governor's action along with support of but one house of congress reversing the executive action of a president was set into the law in 1982. In 1983, the United States supreme court ruled in Immigration and Naturalization Service v. Chadha that legislative vetoes of executive branch actions constituted a clear violation of constitutional provisions for the passage of legislation. Congress is supposed to pass legislation and when it is signed by the president, they are done with their role in the process.

Any reasonable reading of Chadha (a 7-2 supreme court ruling) would lead to a conclusion that the action by the governor of Nevada and the override actions by congress are contrary to the Constitution. So, in final analysis, the matter may be settled in the courts.

Nevada leaders have vowed to fight to the end. If the governor's veto is overridden, Nevada will have a case, but it will be a difficult one. The state will be burdened with showing that the unconstitutional veto process in the 1982 Act is so onerous that it voids the entire act, and hence voids the selection of Yucca Mountain for waste storage.

However, in the unlikely event that the governor's veto is sustained, the president will have the easier task of showing only that the provision for the governor's veto and the congressional override is unconstitutional, and that the selection of Nevada for the waste site was validated at the moment the president made the selection.

Either way, the notion of nullification would be negated by a court ruling. And for this Nevadan, that is just as well. What with "quicky" divorces, brothels, grocery store slot machines, Howard Hughes, Meyer Lansky, and Bugsy Siegel, we have enough of a legacy to live with. It would be simply awful if we had to be joined together in the legacy of John C. Calhoun, Ross Barnett, and George Wallace as well.

HNN, April 29, 2002

27. Two Things Nevada Can Be Proud of: Put Them on the Coin

This commentary concerns the new 25 cent coins celebrating events of each of the states of our union. I take what some might mistakenly consider a "parochial" perspective, as I discuss the portrayals I desire to see on the Nevada coin when it is minted.

Each day we should celebrate, celebrate as if we just pushed Sisyphus's rock over the mountain, even if we only pushed it up a few feet, even if it slipped out of our hands and all we can show is that we made the effort.

But celebrate we must—especially when we do push the rock over the top. Nevadans will soon be able to celebrate as the U.S. Mint will issue a 25 cent coin, a quarter, commemorating the state of Nevada as part of our federal Union. Appropriately, the coin will be silver plated. But what should be on the two faces of the coin? As a Nevadan I feel impelled to "weigh in" with my suggestions for our state coin.

We are a special state. O.K., every state can claim to be special, I suppose. But at this juncture in time, national political leaders recognize a special feature that has been part of the Nevadan existence since time immemorial—our wide open desert spaces. We have been a geographic void and also at times a political and economic void on our national landscape. Such a fact has driven much of our internal political and economic life. And now such a fact results in a nationally driven policy (made with some disrespect to our state) which will make our state the location for all the nation's nuclear waste. In exchange for this special honor, we must demand that we also be selectively honored by having two sides of a new 25 cent coin devoted to matters we think deserve celebration.

William N. Thompson

Being somewhat of a cynic and contrarian I might suggest some dark humor—maybe a mushroom cloud, a caricature of Joe Conforte and his Mustang Ranch, or an Elvis Wedding chapel. Then we might put a jack-o-lantern and a costume mask in appropriate recognition that a president (Lincoln) chose Halloween (really!) as the day he proclaimed statehood for Nevada. Talk about tricks and treats! Or maybe with a bit more seriousness, we could feature our notable industry figures along with a clock showing dice for hour numbers. We could place the profiles of Bugsy Siegel, Meyer Lansky, Howard Hughes, or the latter day Steve Wynn and Sheldon Adelson on the coin. But I won't make such suggestions.

Instead I will be very serious. Our state has very serious things to celebrate. We are the Battleborn State, for among all the others, we were given a place in the union in order to save and preserve our national Union at a time of Civil War. We were proclaimed to be a state in 1864, one week before the national election. Lincoln thought he needed more electoral votes, and we helped reelect the president and his "Union" ticket. Statehood was seen as a reward for the fact that the mines of our state afforded the nation great wealth that was used to successfully prosecute the Civil War. While the Territory of Nevada lacked the requisite population to justify becoming a state, Lincoln and congress promoted the notion as a way of mustering extra needed support for war policies and for anti-slavery and civil rights amendments to the U.S. Constitution.

The new state legislature met in December 1864 and elected William M. Stewart and James W. Nye as the first two U.S. Senators from Nevada. H. C. Hollingsworth had been elected the first member of the U.S. house of representatives in the November election. The three rushed to Washington where they voted in favor of the constitutional proposal (13th Amendment) to end slavery. In January the measure was sent to the states for ratification and the Nevada legislature ratified the amendment on February 16, 1865. The state and its delegation was also important for the proposing and ratification of the 14th and 15th amendments. Nevada was the first state to ratify the Fifteenth. We must always celebrate the fact that the existence of Nevada means national union and freedom. Appropriate events from the 1860s should be placed on one side of the new coin.

On the other side of the coin we should recognize a recent event that still cries out for a celebration that never was held. For reasons stated above, I should never apologize for seriously offering this idea: the State of Nevada and the nation should now join in celebrating the stunning accomplishment of the 1990 UNLV Running Rebels basketball team led my coach Jerry Tarkanian and his cadre of all American players.

It is funny that any small Iowa farm town will place a sign at its borders proclaiming that its high school girls softball team won the class C regional title in 1983. And the sign is still there. However, the interpersonal battles between a university president and a coach stopped Las Vegas and Nevada from having a real celebration after a victory unmatched in American college sports history. No where in Las Vegas is there now (or has there even been) a publicly visible sign saying we won the national basketball championship. Instead of celebrating, we retrenched and held but a singular rally in which we shouted out one word—"Repeat." Ergo we stood as if we were losers and cried out "Wait until next year."

But alas, there was no "next year," we were UNLV, not UCLA, we did not "repeat." We keep waiting, and we keep retreating into the malaise that is an inferiority complex—a sense we are losers—that has gripped the state through most of its history. We very much need to break this cycle, our state desperately needs a celebration, and what the 1990 team accomplished in the sports world was so big, that we can still celebrate—it was so big that we must celebrate. If we never do, we may always be clinging to the notion that we are losers.

But Nevadans are not losers. We are a state that helped win a civil war that restored our national unity, we are a state that helped achieve the political victory that ended the scourge of slavery in our midst, we won freedom. Our state is a state of victories. Our state is the state of champions. Let us celebrate those victories and championships on our new national coin.

This celebration will be a celebration we can personally "own." This celebration will encompass the spirit of celebration that will preclude others from coopting our loyalties in a way that may endanger our liberty. Basketball, cheering crowds, and Freedom: Celebrations for Nevada's 25 cent coin.

HNN, March 18, 2002

28. Moralistic Politics Die in California

The notion of political cultures (or subcultures) holding influence over political activity became part of the literature of Political Science in the 1960s. Especially influential was the work of Daniel Elazar who saw three cultures dominating state politics: the Traditional culture, the Individualistic culture, and the Moralistic culture. (Elazar, Daniel. 1966. American Federalism: A View from the States. New York: Crowell).

In the Traditional culture, political actors seek to preserve the status quo on behalf of the power interests that dominate society. The apartheid Old South provided the most apparent examples of this culture.

The Individualistic culture saw politicians as brokers among competing interests. Politics was a vocation similar to horse trading, and after the political battles were fought, the landscape was filled with winners and losers. Government was a giant zero-sum game. The Individualistic pattern was the most prevalent one across America, but it dominated in political machine states such as Illinois, New York, and Pennsylvania.

In the Moralistic culture, the political actors do not hold their fingers in the political winds lowering their hands only for campaign contributions. Rather they pursue the "good" as their hearts and souls direct them to do. Political arguments involving finding the path to the higher good for society, a good that makes all the members of the society winners. Moralistic states included Minnesota, Connecticut, Oregon, and California—the proto-typical Moralistic state.

In the mining and railroad eras, California was dominated by many selfish interests. However, California was the Golden State as it ushered in the politics of the Progressive and Populist eras. Hiram Johnson was the major doorkeeper. Johnson made the power of the railroads his major campaign issue as he won the governorship in

1910. Upon taking office, one journalist said, "It was as if the whole state of California, having let its government go to pot for half a century, abruptly dropped everything for a mass spasm of civil house cleaning and rehabilitation." (Culver, J and Shelly, L. 1997. Politics and Public Policy in California. New York: McGraw Hill, p.22). The "spasm" did not cease for the next seventy years.

Johnson was followed by giants the likes of Earl Warren, Goodwin Knight, Edmund "Pat" Brown, and even a conservative Ronald Reagan who maintained the notion of politics as a "higher calling" for achieving a better society. For the most part the legacy of reform and moralistic politics encompassed policies either banning or severely restricting legalized (and illegal) gambling. But oh! How things have changed in the past two decades.

Hiram Johnson included anti-gambling fever in his progressive reforms. In 1911 he signed legislation to prohibit race track gambling and to ban slot machines. Earl Warren faced gambling operations that were often under the control of organized crime interests. He helped push operators to Nevada as well.

One of Earl Warren's first acts as state attorney general was to shut down illegal dog tracks, gambling speakeasies, and bookmaking operations. As governor in 1939, Warren took on Tony Stralla, a notorious rumrunner and underworld figure with connections to Al Capone's organization. Warren closed boats Stralla ran off the coast of Santa Monica. Stralla was soon on the Las Vegas Strip as operator of the new Stardust casino resort. Warren admitted that he had an "ingrained bias against commercialized gambling." He called it "corruptive, dishonest in operation, and often cruel in its consequences." (White, G. 1982. Earl Warren: A Public Life. Oxford: Oxford University Press, p. 51).

California was not without gambling. Parimutuel horse racing had been legalized in 1933, there were charitable bingo games, and since the Gold Rush days poker parlors where players competed against one another had survived legal challenges. In the modern era one of these parlors—the Bicycle Club in Bell Gardens—actually had the largest table gaming area in the world for a time. When Governors Johnson, Warren, the Browns (Edmund and his son, Governor Jerry Brown), Reagan, George Deukmejian, and Pete Wilson reached out against gambling, they actually were putting forth notions not accepted by majority sentiment in the state. Estimates have suggested a large part of the gambling activity in Nevada was by Californians. (Dombrink, J. and Thompson, W. 1990. The Last Resort: Success and Failure in Campaigns for Casinos. Reno: University of nevada Press, p. 162; see also Dunstan, R. 1997. Gambling in California. Sacramento: California State Library).

Starting in the 1970s and continuing to this day there have been campaigns for commercial casinos which have been opposed by governors and other leading political actors. (Dombrink and Thompson, p. 163). However, this opposition has become moot to a large extent as casinos have been established on Native American lands, and a lottery has reached into every community in the state.

Native American gambling began as tribes conducted games under the provisions of state charitable gambling rules. However, in the early 1980s the tribes imitated practices of the Seminoles of Hollywood, Florida. They began to violate state rules on prize limits, and such rules as ones governing the time when games could be held. Local government officials sought to stop the games, however, federal courts ruled that the state could only stop the games if the games were criminally illegal per se, and they could not stop them if they were merely being operated in violation of civil regulations. The games on the small Cabazon rancheria east of Los Angeles presented a case situation that eventually reached the U.S.Supreme Court. The high court's ruling upheld earlier rulings and provided the stimulus for passage of the Indian Gaming Regulatory Act of 1988 (IGRA).

The IGRA provided for states and tribes to enter into compacts to regulate casino type gambling if that type of gambling was permitted in any form for any purpose in the state. The California tribes pointed to the state lottery and other existing gambling in the state—poker halls, charitable games, and parimutuel games—and asserted that casino games were permitted. Governors George

Deukmejian and Pete Wilson declined to negotiate compacts. However, as enforcement of gambling laws on tribal lands was in the hands of the federal government, governors could not close tribal casinos.

The change of the cultural environment of California politics was not witnessed first with Native American casinos but with the lottery campaign of 1984. There had been campaigns for commercial casinos, however, after the 1978 adoption of tax limits, public attitudes shifted. Proposition 13 severely affected the opportunities of the state and its local governments to finance public services, especially education. The people were given another chance to make policy on public revenues in 1984. They could establish a lottery and given the state "free" money for education.

The lottery issue had come up before. In 1964 interests placed the question of a privately-run lottery on the ballot. Governor Pat Brown opposed it as trading "on human weakness." The measure failed; 69 percent said "No." In next two decades six more proposals were advanced for lotteries. Only the one in 1984 reached the ballot stage. In 1982 a lottery proposal failed in the legislature. The next year polls showed that the public wanted a lottery as an alternative to having budget cuts or new taxes.

The 1984 campaign was promoted by Scientific Games, a company that manufactured lottery tickets. Scientific Games wrote the ballot proposition. It called for the lottery to start within 135 days, and it had to have an instant game with tickets of certain specifications. Only Scientific Games made the tickets. All officers of supply companies had to make full income disclosures. Only Scientific Games officials had done so because it was a subsidiary of Bally's Casinos. Bally's was required to make the disclosures for casino licensing. Lottery funds were for education. Scientific Games recruited teachers to circulate petitions. The company invested two million dollars in the campaign. The proposition assured the public that the lottery was not going to lead to "bad" gambling. It banned casino games. The public was not informed that Bally's was about to purchase the large M.G.M. casinos in Nevada. The proposal protected Bally's from casino competition from California.

The lottery was opposed by the governor, the attorney general, and local school boards. They felt lotteries would draw revenues mostly from poor persons. Money won. The measure passed with 58 percent voting "Yes." Scientific Games won a first year contract for instant tickets unopposed. The contract was for $40 million. Education received lottery funding, but the legislature cut other funding for education so the total school budgets did not change much.

The new public sentiment was also reflected in votes favoring Native American casinos. In the early 1980s tribes ran charity games such as bingo. To gain a competitive advantage over other charities, tribes chose to ignore state rules regulating hours and prize limits. Local officials tried to stop the violations, but federal courts ruled that the state could only stop games if they were criminally illegal per se, not if they were merely operated in violation of regulations. The rulings led Congress to pass the Indian Gaming Regulatory Act of 1988 (IGRA). The IGRA allowed states and tribes to enter into compacts to regulate casino gambling if that gambling was permitted in any form in the state. California officials balked at making compacts with tribes that now wanted slot machines and casino games. Tribes started the games anyway.

As enforcement of gambling on tribal lands was by the federal government (in accordance with the IGRA), state governors could not close the casinos. U.S. Attorney General Janet Reno judiciously decided not to authorize more raids after "Waco." Desiring legal status, the tribes sponsored legislative initiative Proposition 5 in 1998. It authorized unlimited and unregulated (by outsiders) casinos on the tribal lands—California has over 100 tribes. The tribes put almost $70 million into the campaign—one tribe—the San Manual in San Bernardino—contributed $26 million. Nevada casinos responded with $25 million in opposition. This was the most expensive political race in American history with the exception of the last three presidential races. Money won. Voters gave the proposition over 60 percent approval.

However, the proposition was in the form of a legislative initiative, and the courts found it unconstitutional. Nevada casinos paid for the court challenge, using the 1984 lottery provision to stop the casinos. The tribes regathered and lobbied new Governor Gray Davis for support of a constitutional initiative—Proposition 1A—to allow casinos. He helped write the proposition. The measure limits individual tribes to casinos with up to 2000 slot machines as well as traditional casino games. It provides for some state regulations and taxation. Nevada interests, stung by the amount of money that the tribes were willing to spend in 1998, were content with the new provisions. They were pleased not to have to spend money against casinos again—a position that made them feel hypocritical.

In the formerly Moralistic state of California, gambling has ceased to be seen as an activity that can harm people or compromise moral values. Rather it is seen in terms of money—who gets the money and who doesn't get the money. An unsuspecting public easily neglects the source of gambling dollars (their own pockets) as it is drawn to appeals from those who will receive the money—the government treasurers and tribes who collect the funds. They are playing a win-lose game mandated by the new culture of California. Only in a game with selfish outcomes will political interests—California tribes and Nevada casinos—invest nearly a hundred million dollars in a political referendum campaign. Where is the golden beacon at the top of the hill? Where is the Golden State?

This essay combines materials from HNN, June 17 and June 25, 2001

29. Jeffords Bad, Jeffords Good: A Partisan Republican View

As a Republican I share the feelings of losing once again, the feelings of once again being slapped in the face for identifying with the party of "bible thumpers" and Attila the Hun. It was a defeat to have Senator Jeffords leave the party. It was a defeat to lose control of the senate. I do not want to play any "sour grapes" role, however, by reflecting on the good that could come from the change. Quite frankly, as the story unfolded, I (like many other Republicans) wished and wished that a Democrat or two (Miller, Breaux, or perhaps Nelson) would switch the other way. But that isn't to be, and realistically, the Democrats are likely to have an even stronger majority within the next year if either Senators Thurmond or Helms have to leave public life "prematurely." The Republicans lost—I admit it. But then, just maybe, they also won, and maybe President George W. Bush also won. I'll return to my Republican perspective in a moment.

First, I wish to add that as an American, I am very content that Senator Strom Thurmond is no longer the president pro tempore of the Senate—that he is no longer third in line for the presidency in case some unthinkable multiple disaster could strike our leadership. It is much better that the much younger Democrat, Senator Robert Byrd, take over this role. If thrust into the role of the presidency, at least Byrd would not have to come out of a coma in order to select a new vice president (we'd just have to get Gore out of the Pizza Hut).

Second, as a Nevadan, I am thoroughly delighted with the results of the Jeffords switch. As a small state (two million people), Nevada now has the second most powerful Senator—majority whip Harry Reid. Party doesn't really count all that much in Nevada. Our state's (commercial) interest always come first whether we have a liberal Democrat like Reid representing us or a conservative Republican like Senator John Ensign. We have some big big issues on which Senator Reid's new "clout" can be a controlling factor in our favor. Consider that Reid engineered the Jeffords move. He negotiated the quid pro quo which gave the new Independent the chair of the environmental committee in the senate, and I trust he assured Jeffords that in the future Vermont will be favored in all policy decisions made by the senate. Jeffords must be grateful and so too must every other Democrat in the senate. It is inconceivable that in this political milieu, Mc McCain can be successful in his efforts to hurt our state's basic industry by banning all gambling bets on college sports events. It is inconceivable also that action will be taken to impose an unwanted nuclear waste repository on Nevada lands. Such a facility that would require that nuclear waste shipments move near our resort corridor or mingle with resort traffic every day. As a Republican I am dismayed, as a Nevadan I am happy about Jeffords switch move.

But let me return to my Republican perspective. The Jeffords switch is not good in the sense that the party lost a moderate liberal voice. Liberals belong in the Republican Party—it is the party of Abraham Lincoln—the "Freedom" Party. And it is the party of the one president since Lincoln that did the most to honor the Thirteenth Amendment—Richard Nixon. The "liberal" in me (and the father in me) must forever be thankful that a Republican President Nixon (against Democrat opposition) ended the draft. My children and all other citizens can now heed the call for service without being forced to do so by threat of jail or having to freeze in the Canadian tundra.

But I see advantages for President Bush in the move. He will be helped by facing opposition party control in the senate. First of all, Bush now has an opportunity to be held "responsible," and that is one of his themes that I support. His campaign claim was that he was a person who could build bridges to his opponents. He claimed to have done so in Texas, now we can see if he produces in Washington. With Republican majorities in both houses, he did not have an opportunity to prove himself. The change is good for him. Just think of the accolades he would be enjoying now if he had pushed the tax and budget plan through an opposition led senate. Now think of his victories if energy reform or education reform passes congress. Bush wants to deal with issues. Now the Democrats can put the issues on the open plate and we can see full debates on a patient's bill of rights, senior drugs, and campaign finance reform. And if Bush can engineer meaningful compromises, he can win credit, if he can't, he can take responsibility. The same goes for Daschle and Reid—they too have to produce—that means dropping the "rich man poor man" "you're stupid" mantra we've heard for the past five months.

Having majorities in congress has not been all that good for presidents in the past. Kennedy was stymied in his relationships with a Democrat congress. Lyndon Johnson was considered a "great legislator" but all he really had was a flock of Democrat sheep that gave us a bureaucratic policy disaster called the "War on Poverty" and then acquiesced in support for Mr. MacNamara's war.

On the other hand Democrat President Truman thrived with a congress against him. He scored public victories by opposing the "Do Nothing Congress" of Republicans. Republican President Eisenhower floundered with Republican majorities and Joe McCarthy in congress. However, toward the end of his tenure, his party suffered disastrous congressional losses in 1958, and Eisenhower then demonstrated his greatest strength as a political leader. And of course, Clinton was a eunuch when the Democrats controlled congress. But once Republicans Gingrich and Lott took over Clinton became the poster child for virility. A man that stood for nothing flourished because he stood against congress.

Moreover, Bush has been taken off the hook. He can now espouse social conservative views such as the "faith based" thing and anti-abortion policies, but he doesn't have to produce. He might actually send some strong anti-abortion judicial candidates forth, and he can then take credit for doing so. But when the senate bottles up the appointments in committee, he can withdraw them and put forth persons who will be economic conservatives. He can let the Democrats take him off the hook with the far right. He can continue to get their campaign funds and their staunch support, but like Reagan, he can avoid causing policy decisions that the country doesn't want. I guess that isn't the heights of responsibility but then that would be quite acceptable to this Republican. The Jeffords switch ain't all that bad for the new President.

TP, June 10, 2001

Parables from (a not quite) Paradise, NV 89154

30. Pork Barrel Comes to White Pine County—My Day With the Senator

...Casting a bit of doubt on that phrase, "It is more blessed to give..."

Nevada's Chic Hecht won an upset election to the United States senate in 1982 by defeating twenty-four year incumbent Howard Cannon. Hecht, the owner of a retail clothing store in Las Vegas, fashioned himself as a spokesman for small businessmen. Actually, in the campaign he didn't speak at all, as his campaign surrogates hit Cannon hard on a series of negatives that had been brought forth in various federal investigations. In congress the senator set about to establish himself as a staunch conservative. He proudly pointed out that his voting record was the second most conservative one in the body. The most conservative senator was James McClure of Idaho. Senator Hecht liked to refer to his Republican colleague Senator Helms, as "My liberal friend Jesse." (Helms was the third most conservative member of the senate.)

Senator Hecht prided himself on being close to the people. During each of his years in office, he took his entire Washington staff on a tour of the small cities and towns of remote rural Nevada. Nevertheless there was one part of the "liberal" Washington scene that affected Hecht as it did other Republicans. The good senator did not at all mind seeing the federal dollar being spent—if it were being spent in his state. Certainly Nevada had been receiving its share of federal dollars for various projects, and the senator was happy to present the checks.

I was invited to accompany Senator Hecht on the first leg of his tour as our Center for Business and Economic Research at the University of Nevada, Las Vegas was working with him analyzing policies for small businesses. I was serving as the associate director of the Center. As the tour (three cars) was reaching Ely, Nevada, birthplace of Pat (Thelma Ryan) Nixon and seat of White Pine County, the senator was delighted that he was carrying a message that good "Ole Uncle Sam" was not forgetting White Pine County at the pork barrel trough.

A special meeting of the county commission had been convened so that Senator Hecht could exchange views "one on one" with the good commissioners, small business persons, and citizens of White Pine. After he made his most important announcement about his delivery of "Pork," he found out that matters were not exactly "one on one." The conservative was to learn another thing or two about federal spending.

The scene is the White Pine County Courthouse, Ely, Nevada, Wednesday August 29, 1984. It is 8:50 p.m. The Senator has engaged those present with fifty minutes of give and take on a variety of questions, mostly involving either very general philosophical matters of politics or very individual personal concerns re matters such as last week's social security check. It has already been a very long day for the senator. But the day is not over.

Bill Farr, the senator's chief staff member from his Reno office, rose up. Farr, who himself had been a county commission chair, addressed the gathering. "This morning, the Senator met with Al Stone of the Department of Transportation in Las Vegas. They had a long discussion. After the discussion the Senator was happy to tell Stone that he would make this announcement tonight here in Ely. Senator, would you like to make the announcement now."

Senator Hecht spoke, "Al Stone of the Department of Transportation of the state of Nevada has informed me…let me see…it is kind of hard to read his writing…yes, the federal government has asked the state to release its allocated highway funds, $5,348,000, for the improvements on the Sunnyside cutoff of state route 318. He indicates that most of these funds will be coming into White Pine County."

Murmurs were heard throughout the audience, and the commissioners were ready to speak for the assembled group. The commission chair, Dr. Kendall Jones, led off.

"Sometimes when I hear about these federal highway funds and the state Department of Transportation, I wish we could secede from the state of Nevada, and be annexed to Utah, or become a state by ourselves. It's always $1.2 million or $5.5 million that will benefit White Pine County. Really it's money to improve the transportation for people who go from Utah or Idaho to Las Vegas, or Salt Lake City to Reno. It really doesn't do a hell of a lot for the economy of this county. These highway contracts are let out to construction concerns that are not located in White Pine County. Employees, about 80% are from outside White Pine County. Equipment is purchased outside of White Pine County. The materials, the depreciation, everything else is not a factor in this economy. And if we get out of our $1.6 million on this last transportation contract we had, if White Pine County benefits by $200,000 actually into this economy of White Pine County, we are lucky, very lucky. Because those people who are employed, their families stay in Las Vegas where they live, and the money they spend is in Las Vegas, the supplies are purchased in Las Vegas, the depreciation, the taxes, all go to Las Vegas. They don't come to White Pine County."

Staffer Farr sought to rescue the beleaguered Hecht. He spoke, "I'm not debating that. I'm just trying to bring a message to you, I want to indicate to you, I thought it was very kind of Stone to indicate that those funds are coming to this county. As a spin-off of those dollars that are here, if you want to talk economics. When those people are here we can talk about generating state taxes that do help throughout the state of Nevada. I wouldn't take a total negative attitude. We are not getting into a debate with the state. We are here carrying a message to you."

The feathers of county commissioner Brent Elderidge were not smoothed. "In the past the federal highway dollars have gone a long way to building secondary roads of regional significance. I live on one. We were informed two months ago that we will become the proud owners of the worn out highway. And we have to take care of the maintenance of the road. And now we have an announcement that the federal government is going to go into building highways of statewide significance. It doesn't do much for me personally. I feel that White Pine County as the county of the state that is going to receive most of the worn out roads is getting the short end of the stick. Any industry we bring in will be hindered and held back by damn poor roads. And our roads are being built for tourists that pass through. I don't say I'm against tourists."

Farr tried again. "I don't propose that I represent Al Stone. This morning Al met with the senator. When he heard the senator was coming to Ely, he handwrote a little message for you. I would not hesitate to bring that message to you. Even taking the brunt. As a former county commissioner, I know what you're up against. I've had that experience. But nonetheless, I wouldn't be totally negative about it, those dollars have to go someplace. I'm glad they're going to White Pine County, as a citizen."

Elderidge put in the final words. "When federal dollars came in the past, was there any restriction that they had to stay roads forever. Or is it the state's discretion to say, here county, here's your road. Do you know?" There was no response, and Elder concluded, "Will I think you should find out."

Senator Hecht stood up again, and spoke. "Let's go to some other questions where we can help. Problems we can help with, that's what we're here for."

31. Red, White, and Blue, From Sea to Shining Sea, Long May It Wave

As a gambling researcher in Las Vegas, I am often called upon to comment on the many maladies that afflict the social fabric of my community. I do so recognizing one major disconnect. Over 5000 vote each month with their feet. Their votes say Las Vegas has to be doing something right because they move here. They make us the fastest growing community in the country. Often I think we should have a day to celebrate good things about Las Vegas. We don't.

People of the world vote with their feet too. They choose to come to America more than anywhere else. Fortunately we have a day to celebrate good things about America. We should. I am often a contrarian and a cynic about public policy in my country, but I shall not be so on July 4th.

As a country music fan for 50 years, I consider Robert Altman's 1975 film "Nashville," to be one of my least favorites of all time. This hideous Hollywood mockery of a popular culture form featured a song entitled "We Must Be Doing Something Right to Last 200 Years." It was a terrible song, performed in a manner to insult anyone who has enjoyed country music; yet, it carried a message that deserves some reflection. May I suggest a revised title, "We Must Be Doing Something Right to Last 225 Years?" May I suggest that on this one day of the year we identify that thing and those things that we as a nation are doing right.

Isabel Cespedes lives in Queens. She came to the United States with her husband Samuel 30 years ago from Colombia. She thinks America is doing something right. One thing she quickly mentions. No matter who you are, rich or poor, black or white, when you go to a grocery store you stand in line, and the first in line gets served first, no matter who they are.

Shirley Tomovic lives in Niagara Falls, Ontario. Her parents moved to Canada from Europe after the Second World War. Her uncles and brothers have moved to the United States and they all celebrate Freedom Days together (July 1-July 4). She boasts that United States is the best neighbor that Canada or any nation could possibly have. Her family recognizes the great opportunity that comes with liberty in the United States—the freedom to pursue choices in life are available more here than elsewhere. A fantastic sense of openness allows people to seek individual goals. People have a sense of controlling their own destinies.

This propels many to find aggressive business ventures that lead toward wealth, but not just a wealth they selfishly keep to themselves. The pursuit of the choice for wealth is effective because of something derided as "trickle down." It is not that, but rather it is a cascade as if a meteorite shower bringing increased value to a vast overwhelming majority of the American people. This spread of wealth is not some zero sum game, but for 225 years (plus) it has been a positive sum game, a game where all can be winners. And so the vast majority gain a personal sense of controlling their own destinies, and so here more than anywhere else, masses of people feel good about themselves and they feel good about life. Love of self is part of America, and it is not bad.

Because we have personal confidence, respect and love for ourselves, we have a collective confidence that allows us to feel good about others, to love others, and to help others, to voluntarily help others. One of the right things about America is that Americans give freely and openly of their time, their wealth, and indeed even of their lives to help others.

In 1861 at the age of 29 my great great uncle Richard Thompson left his wife and three children to join the Illinois Volunteers and march off to Tennessee so that freedom could be expanded and slavery ended. He fell in the Battle of Nashville. And so too in 1967 when he was called, a twenty-two year old, Ronald Colwell of Samaria, Michigan willingly answered and embraced

Army life becoming an officer before he left for southeast Asia, before giving everything.

    Bob Bush gave in Viet Nam and he came back. He has decided that he should not stop giving. He is a builder, but he spends much time with Habitat for Humanity. His wife's family came north from Mexico to Las Vegas where the two met. She handles one job for pay, but many jobs out of love for others in her church Family Assistance Center, with the Boys Club, and the Girls Club. She also recruits volunteers. If you're in Las Vegas and want to offer a helping hand, she'll place you, just call up www.debbiebush.com for a list of opportunities.

    Samuel and Isabel Cespedes' daughter Carmenza graduated from City University with a business degree and decided that she could postpone her personal quest for wealth. She joined the Peace Corps and went to Changinola, Panama where she worked with local women to help them develop an "American-type" entrepreneurial spirit in order to market their craft products effectively for profits. She now works in Brooklyn for Accion assisting small businesses with micro-loans. One loan recipient is a businessman from Libya. He loves America, because here he can really love and respect his customers, many of whom are Jewish. He tells her that in his old land he would have to hate these people, but these people are making his life a success, so he is happy to love them.

    Those that give take a risk, and that is a good thing that is part of the fabric of America. It is ingrained in our people as the vast majority of those here were somewhere else before, and they suffered many risks to be here. So too do people who move from one location to another within our country in a quest to better themselves, and in turn to better their communities. People strive for change to be better, and so too they encourage their country to change for the better also.

    We are a nation of many other nations, but we are not just a melting pot, we are also a mosaic of peoples. In another country peoples from other places like the Cespedes family—which still speaks Spanish in their home—would be Colombians. Here they are that but they are also Americans. I get the same sense about people riding the R train to Manhattan. They have a look suggesting they are so many nationalities, but they are acting the same—rushing about, boarding, standing, taking seats, exiting the train—they are acting as Americans.

Our country celebrates the American peoples from the whole world in its music, in its literature, and its life styles. Twenty-five years ago, July 4th fell on a Sunday. I attended services at the Westwood United Methodist Church in Kalamazoo. It was bicentennial day. But we did not sing "God Bless America;" maybe pastor Alan McCreedy felt that would be provincial. We didn't sing "America the Beautiful;" maybe he felt that would be a bit haughty. We didn't sing "The Star Spangled Banner;" I don't think Alan relished lines about bombs bursting in air. We did sing "Finlandia," by Sibelius. I was taken aback, and I was a little disappointed. But as I have been preparing this column, I have thought about it again, and I think that it is a good song to sing on July 4. Maybe that song is our national anthem too. It tells of a beautiful land with blue skies and wonderful people who love their land; but then it also tells that other countries are beautiful, and that other people love their lands too. And so it is that Americans can look toward the beauty of the entire world, and the wonderful peoples of other lands who love their lands still, even though they came to America for respect, freedom, openness, opportunity to be better, and opportunity to do better for others.

We've lasted 225 years. We are doing a lot of things right. But you ask, does this mean we are perfect? It's July 4, you're damn right we're perfect!

HNN, July 1, 2001

32. God's Grace

All my goodness lies with friends I know
Ones who give kindness everywhere that they go
Ones who stick with me whenever I am low
The one who shares joy with her special glow
All my goodness lies with friends I know

My goodness springs from work of children's hands
From a son helping others in a far distant land
A daughter counselling poor souls toward better plans
A boy giving the world music with a guitar and a band
My goodness springs from work of children's hands

My goodness is reflection of things others do
Without their devotion skies could not be blue
Rivers would run backwards the moon could not be new
We'd just be lonely creatures as if caged in a zoo
My goodness is reflection of God's grace and you

William Thompson is a native of Ann Arbor, Michigan. He received college degrees in Political Science from Michigan State University (B.A., M.A.) and the University of Missouri in Columbia (Ph.D.). He is now a Professor of Public Administration at the University of Nevada, Las Vegas. He has been in Las Vegas since 1980 with his wife of 38 years, Kay. They have three children, Laura, Steve and Tim.

This is the author's eleventh book. He has also written Parables from (a not quite) Paradise, NV. 89154, v. 1: The Nevada Public Radio Commentaries (1stBooks). He coauthored Over The Top: Solutions to the Sisyphus Dilemma of Life (with Bradley Kenny) and Heartlines and Lyrics from Billy Gamble (with Anthony J. Juliano) –both are from 1st Books. His other books include The Last Resort; Success and Failure in Campaigns for Casinos (with John Dombrink), Casino Customer Service (with Michelle Comeau), Legalized Gambling: A Reference Handbook, Native American Issues: A Reference Handbook, and Gambling in America: An Encyclopedia of History, Issues, and Society, International Casino Law (with Anthony Cabot, Andrew Tottenham, and Carl Braunlich), and State Attorneys General and the Environment (With Bradley Smith). To secure his books search www.1stbooks.com. and www.billygamble.com. Most are also in stock at the Gambler's Book Club in Las Vegas. His full biography is available at www.billygamble.com.

The Author

CPSIA information can be obtained
at www.ICGtesting.com
Printed in the USA
FFOW02n0905250417
34937FF